BOWMAN LIBRARY.
MENLO SCHOOL AND MENLO COLLEGE

Dante Commentaries

DANTE
commentaries

Eight Studies
of the
Divine Comedy

Edited by David Nolan

Published for
University College, Dublin
and the
Italian Cultural Institute, Dublin

IRISH ACADEMIC PRESS, DUBLIN
ROWMAN AND LITTLEFIELD, TOTOWA, N.J.

FIRST PUBLISHED BY IRISH ACADEMIC PRESS

3 SERPENTINE AVENUE DUBLIN 4 IRELAND 1977

ISBN 0 7165 2320 5 (cloth)

ISBN 0 7165 2321 3 (paper)

FIRST PUBLISHED IN THE UNITED STATES 1977

BY ROWMAN AND LITTLEFIELD, TOTOWA, N. J.

ISBN 0 87471 966 6

©1977 David Nolan and the individual authors
© All forms of micro publishing

Printed in The Republic of Ireland
by Folens & Co. Dublin

To all who took part in the series of Lecturae Dantis *at University* *College Dublin* *1972-1977*

Contents

Introduction

The first public demonstration of the interest at University College in Dante studies was the invitation to Professor Grayson to lecture there on Dante's poetics in 1971. That lecture, later published in Italian[1], was in its subject matter an appropriate prologue to the four seasons of Dante readings that were to ensue: a series on the *Inferno* in 1972, followed in the succeeding academic year by the *Paradiso,* both promoted by Professor Almansi, and succeeded by a second group of *Inferno* readings in 1975 and by a series on the *Purgatorio* in 1976 with the support of Professor O'Doherty.

On the other hand, successive directors of the Italian Cultural Institute in Dublin have since its foundation in 1954 shown a great interest in Dante studies and have invited some well-known scholars, among others, Professor Getto,[2] to lecture on Dante. In addition the Institute published a volume of essays to honour the seventh centenary of Dante's birth in 1965.[3]

The Institute fully supported the decision by University College to introduce public *Lecturae Dantis.* H.E. the Italian Ambassador, Goffredo Biondi Morra, Principe di San Martino, inaugurated the first series in 1972 and again introduced the 1974 readings. The Director of the Institute Dr. Forti opened the 1975 lectures and also spoke in 1976 at the closing of the series.

Of the lecturers not included in this volume, Professor Limentani and Dr. Boyde from Cambridge took part in the first *Inferno* series; Professor Almansi himself and members of the U.C.D. Department of Italian, Dr. Merry, Dr. O'Grady and Miss Petrie have also contributed over the years, as have Mr. Smith from Bath and Mr. Wilkin from Strathclyde.[4]

But there have been other contributions to Dante studies in Dublin. The first integral translation of the *Divina Commedia* into English by Henry Boyd appeared in Dublin in 1802. Bad though Boyd's verse and mistranslation may now appear, his achievement may have perhaps stimulated Henry Cary to produce his widely influential version shortly afterwards in 1814.[5] And the influence of Dante from then on became more and more insistent among English writers from Keats to Eliot.

Some one hundred and fifty years later, the first volume of the translation into Irish by the late Monsignor Pádraig de Brún was published in Dublin[6] and at the Italian Institute Professor Ó Cuív gave an appreciation of that translation which was published in the Institute's centenary volume.[7] Professor Getto's lectures on behalf of the Institute and at Trinity College, were also published later in his studies on the *veltro,* on the poetry of the *Paradiso* and on Dante's examination by the apostles Peter, James and John.[8] Fr. Foster lectured at Trinity College on Dante, and Professor Brown on the battle of Montaperti at the Institute. Professor McWilliam published his commentary on *Inferno* canto i in *Hermathena.*[9]

Of the commentaries on *Inferno* i then, only Professor Limentani's detailed many interpretations line by line. Getto suggested that Dante himself was to be identified in the *veltro,* and McWilliam linked Dante with Yeats by seeing the *veltro* to mean the second coming. Later Boyde illustrated the beguilement of Francesca, who uses the *stil novo* precepts and language to implicate Dante, by a tapestry of language based on his early poetry, in the doom towards which the love poet's tenets inexorably are seen to lead. He also discussed the presence of Dante author and character in *Inferno* v and their eventual coalescence in the poem.

The early cantos of the poem are not illustrated in this volume, but the readings published here range from Hell to paradise.

From the pinnacle of Heaven Beatrice looks down to judge Simon Magus, chief of simoniacs, and Boniface VIII, who is awaited in that circle of punishment. This is the scope of the present collection: for J. A. Scott ends his commentary on *Paradiso* xxx with a backward view of the simoniacs and the opening reading is of those simoniacs in *Inferno* xix, the canto of the damned popes.

Although Professor Singh begins with a disclaimer, he goes on to assess the views of the main commentators on the Ulysses episode in such a way as to enlarge the horizons of interpretation of the searching personality of Ulysses. And he docs justice to the constant work of W. B. Stanford, who in the *Cambridge Journal* 1952, published his most complete treatment of Dante's mythical Ulysses, which he later incorporated in *The Ulysses Theme* (Oxford, 1954, second ed., 1963). Professor Stanford recently lectured in University College on *Inferno* xxvi and published an account of that lecture in the *A TI Journal,* 18, 1976. As he also referred to the figure of Dante's Ulysses in *The Search for Ulysses* published with J. V. Luce in 1974, and as he here publishes an intriguing comment on the siren in *Purgatorio* xix, he may claim certainly to be the longest-practising and most productive Dublin Dantist. Briefly Professor Stanford argues that the *Fortuna Major* may be identified with the *bivium* in the choice of Hercules. As the choice of Hercules was between virtue and vice, the siren exemplifies vice, the "donna santa e presta" (*Purg.*xix.26), virtue.

Ulysses, too, and Ugolino are exemplars of political condemnation, and if, as Mrs. Lonergan says, Dante in the nether regions of Hell portrays contemporary society as a concourse of demons, this would also include Boniface, so soon expected among the simonists. It should be remembered with reference to this view that very few places for the just remain in Heaven as J. A. Scott points out in his commentary on *Paradiso* xxx.

The *Monarchia,* so important in the background to these cantos, emerges even more strongly in the reading of *Paradiso* vi, on Justinian. The whole idea of the Donation of Constantine, "di quanto mal fu matre" (*Inf.*xix.115), overshadows Dante's theories of the Church and Empire. And the textual critic has his moment in J.H. Whitfield's lecture, not to the same extent as Pope's inspired Shakespearean emendation ("'a babbled of green fields"), but with Ricci's recovery of "iustitia" for "instantia", providing bedrock for a sketch that features emperors. Then basing the Romeo identification with Dante on the use of "giusto", Professor Whitfield ties the strands of the canto together.

In his commentary on *Inferno* xxvi, Professor Singh warns of the assumption that there is anything new to say about Dante. The excuse for the present collection, then, is to provide a stimulus for an intelligent reading of Dante and to offer sensible interpretations for English-speaking readers of the *Commedia* that are free from such critical encrustations as jargon and novelty impose. If an audience is attracted that includes other than the master and student in English-speaking institutions of learning, then the collection will have exceeded the expectations of the editor.[10]

Notes

[1] The lecture was published in Italian in Cecil Grayson, *Cinque saggi su Dante* (Bologna, 1972).

[2] Professor Getto also lectured at Trinity College Dublin and in Cork in 1964.

[3] *An Irish Tribute to Dante* (Dublin, 1965). An exhibition of original illustrations of Dante in a competition for a series of prizes was also organized at the Italian Institute for the centenary.

[4] It is hoped the present volume will shortly be followed by the publication of some of their contributions.

[5] For Boyd and Cary, see Gilbert F. Cunningham, *The Divine Comedy in English 1782-1900* (Edinburgh, 1958). The best concise account of the influence of Dante in English is C.P. Brand, "Dante and the English Poets" in *The Mind of Dante,* ed. U. Limentani (Cambridge, 1965), pp. 163-200.

[6] *Coiméide Dhiaga Dante,* Leabhar I, *Ifreann,* Monsignor Pádraig de Brún d'aistrigh (Dublin, 1963).

[7] B. Ó Cuív, "Coiméide Dhiaga Dante", in *An Irish Tribute to Dante* (see note [3]), pp. 1-12.

[8] In for instance Giovanni Getto, *Aspetti della poesia di Dante* (Florence, 1966).

[9] G. H. McWilliam, "Dante's Smooth Beast: A Commentary on the Opening Canto of the *Commedia",* *Hermathena,* 113 (1972), 15-33.

[10] In editing I have used *Commedia* throughout rather than *Comedy;* the capitalization of *Nuova* and *Commedia* in the titles *Vita Nuova* and *Divina Commedia* is also maintained. Abbreviations of Dante's works that are used throughout are *Inf., Purg., Par., Mon., Con., VN, DVE.* Other abbreviations are self-evident where used. Standard classical and medieval references, principally in the readings by Stanford and Scott, are given in accepted abbreviations. References to standard commentators, ancient and modern, are generally given without references in the text, although occasionally an

individual reference is noted in detail as it may refer to a particular edition. The standard modern editions used are such as Casini, Momigliano, Porena, Sapegno, Scartazzini and Vandelli. References to standard translations such as those of Sayers, Sinclair and Ciardi are also not always given in full. The text of the *Commedia* used is that edited by G. Petrocchi, 4 vols (Milan, 1966). For the text of the *Monarchia,* the edition by Pier Giorgio Ricci, *Le opere di Dante Alighieri,* Vol. V, Edizione Nazionale a cura della Società Dantesca (Milan, 1965) has been cited. The *De Vulgari Eloquentia* edition adopted is that by P. V. Mengaldo (Padua, 1968). The *Convivio* is based on the edition by G. Busnelli and G. Vandelli, 2 vols (Florence, 1934-7). References to St. Thomas, St. Augustine, Migne, Du Cange are normally abbreviated. Some short passages taken from Dante, *The Divine Comedy,* 3 vols (London, 1971), translated by John D. Sinclair are published by permission of the Oxford University Press. The editor wishes to acknowledge the work of Dante scholars referred to in these essays but above all he is grateful for the permission of the Società Dantesca to quote from the Dante works published by them.

Inferno XIX

David Nolan

The subject of the papacy and the contemporary Church is one that is central to the development of Dante's *Divina Commedia*. A universal vision of man's destiny and human society naturally dwells on the efficacy of such an important institution and such a responsible authority. If unprepared for, then, St. Peter's statement on the subject in the *Paradiso* would come as a shock. According to St. Peter when Dante meets him, the papal office in 1300 is vacant in the eyes of Heaven. Peter considers that Boniface VIII, who was then the reigning pope, is a usurper and that policies that please the devil have prevailed against the true tradition of the Church.

> 'Quelli ch'usurpa in terra il luogo mio,
>   il luogo mio, il luogo mio che vaca
>   ne la presenza del Figliuol di Dio,
> fatt' ha del cimitero mio cloaca
>   del sangue e de la puzza; onde 'l perverso
>   che cadde di qua sú, là giú si placa.'   *Par.*xxvii.22-7

These lines and Peter's speech that follows in *Paradiso* xxvii.40-66 are a culmination to relentless criticism in the *Divina Commedia* of the contemporary papacy and of corruption in the Church. For before that the allegorical pageant in the earthly paradise in *Purgatorio* xxxii is an extension of the attack on the Church made by Dante out of his own mouth in *Inferno* xix, an attack that is justified by the instructions of Peter to him to speak out and hide nothing (*Par.*xxvii.64-6).[1] The final words of this campaign in the poem against Church corruption may be said to be those pronounced by Beatrice when, speaking of the simonists and referring to Boniface VIII as "quel d'Alagna", she says that Clement V

> . . . sarà detruso
> là dove Simon mago è per suo merto,
> e farà quel d'Alagna intrar piú giuso'.   *Par.*xxx.146-8

She thus prophesies the damnation of Boniface VIII and reinforces the sentence already brought home to the reader much earlier when Nicholas III dramatically mistakes Dante for Boniface in the circle of the simonists in *Inferno* xix.[2]

Of the themes of the *Divina Commedia* then, Church corruption recurs again and again and, of the characters in the poem, Pope Boniface VIII is one of those alluded to most frequently. Avarice is a besetting sin in Dante's world and he sees it as being at the root of Church corruption. The she-wolf of avarice, that first appeared in *Inferno* i.49-51, is later cursed by Dante:

> Maladetta sie tu, antica lupa.   *Purg.*xx.10

This curse follows significantly on an example of avarice in *Purgatorio* xix, Pope Adrian V, in whom Church corruption and the vice were wed.[3] Significantly, too, in the circle of the avaricious in Hell (*Inf.*vii.37-48), in response to Dante's desire to identify individuals among the mass of avaricious clerics,

Virgil explains that they are unrecognizable but that the clerics were

'. . . e papi e cardinali,
in cui usa avarizia il suo soperchio.'   *Inf.*vii.47-8

In the *Monarchia* Dante was to say that avarice was the greatest obstacle to justice. This provides a clue to an understanding of Dante's criticism of the Church. For the *Monarchia* may be taken to be Dante's answer to Boniface's bull *Unam sanctam*. Boniface's bull in 1302 was the classical statement of the doctrine of temporal power for the Church, in which he said that "the spiritual and the temporal swords are in the power of the Church; but the latter must be used for the Church and the former by the Church"; "the one sword, however, must be under the other and the temporal authority subjected to the spiritual power."[4] The *Monarchia* offered a reply to this as there Dante insisted that spiritual power was the only concern of the Church and temporal power the province solely of the Emperor. It outlined the basis of his disapproval of the contemporary papacy as he maintained that the Church should have no temporal power, absolutely none.

Thus the *Monarchia,* though possibly a later formulation of his theories in a projection on to a theoretical plane, provides the basis for understanding the motivation for his handling of avarice and the popes in a narrative and dramatic medium. The indictment of the contemporary Church and of the tradition of the true Church, which Dante delivers in person in *Inferno* xix and which is further developed in *Purgatorio* xxxii by Beatrice and in *Paradiso* xxvii by St. Peter, involves of necessity the condemnation of the papacy and of individual popes. This is particularly true of Boniface throughout the *Commedia* and of the simoniac popes in general in *Inferno* xix.

To Boniface VIII there are many references. He is the object of so much of Dante's *saeva indignatio* that no pope is referred to more often in the *Commedia,* although only in *Inferno* xix is he referred to by name. He was pope from 1294-1303 and replaced St. Celestine V, whom he is reputed to have persuaded to resign.[5] In *Inferno* xxvii Guido da Montefeltro, who had been influenced by Boniface to give fraudulent advice for the purpose of the Pope's political schemes, calls him "lo principe d'i novi Farisei" (*Inf.* xxvii.85), and Dante shows Boniface in an extremely unfavourable light, for he has Guido say that Boniface pardoned him, Guido, for his sin before he committed it. This is highly unlikely of a pope who was in fact a Church lawyer and described by Giovanni Villani as "very learned in the Scriptures" and "a very prudent and able man".[6] Dante's disapproval of the contemporary papacy was motivated by extremely strong feelings of political and religious opposition to Boniface. Dante even showed uncompromising hatred of the great opponent of his conviction that the Church should have no temporal power.

Dante also detested Boniface because he had been forced into exile by the Pope's intervention in the affairs of Florence in 1301. It is this fierce resentment that comes to the surface in *Inferno* xix, as Dante, who wrestles with the difficulty of placing in Hell a living person, solves the problem with a dramatic recognition scene as Pope Nicholas III thinks he is talking to Boniface. Dante goes on to expand his criticism of the individual pope to include Church policy and the papacy of his time. With remarkable self-confidence he pronounces an attack on the papacy and Church that recalls the fulminating zeal of the Old Testament prophets.

But his conviction of the corruption in the contemporary Church and popes is not enough to explain the presence of the simonists in the circle of fraud, for that is where they are. In *Inferno* xix, Dante describes the punishment for the sale of ecclesiastical favours and offices and the gifts of the Holy Spirit known as simony after its first New Testament practitioner, Simon Magus of Samaria. Indeed the opening apostrophe, "O Simon mago" is an address to the particular Simon who left his name to posterity as the first to apply this concept of traffic in holy things to the early Christian Church.[7]

Virgil and Dante have reached the third trench of Malebolge, a realm prefigured in *Inferno* xi by Virgil as containing:

> ipocresia, lusinghe e chi affattura,
> falsità, ladroneccio e simonia,
> ruffian, baratti e simile lordura.   *Inf.*xi.58-60

The best explanation of the placing of the simonists in the circle of fraud is probably that which admits that the practice of simony is not fraudulent in itself. The fraud lies in the deceit practised on the Church by wolves in the guise of shepherds.[8]

The simonists are imagined by Dante as confined underground in fissures of the rock of Malebolge:

> Luogo è in inferno detto Malebolge,
> tutto di pietra di color ferrigno,
> come la cerchia che dintorno il volge.   *Inf.*xviii.1-3

They enter the rock by one of the holes which riddle it but they remain for a time with their legs out, the soles of their feet aflame until a successor comes to take their place and squeeze them further down within the rock. This rock of Malebolge is honeycombed by these parasites who were intent on wealth in their lives. The rock is described as follows:

> Io vidi per le coste e per lo fondo
> piena la pietra livida di fóri,
> d'un largo tutti e ciascun era tondo,
>
>   *Inf.*xix.13-15

and later Dante describes the pit of the *bolgia* as "foracchiato e arto" (42). Throughout the canto Dante harps on the avarice of these prelates for "oro" and "argento", words that are repeated three times at lines 4, 95 and 112.[9]

The reference to Simon's original attempt in the Acts of the Apostles to buy the gift given by God when he approached Peter and John in Samaria and asked them to sell him the ability to bring down the Holy Spirit on those on whom he laid his hands, is parodied in the reverse of the gift that is now bestowed on the simonists, in that tongues of flame lick the soles of their feet in their upturned position. Rather than on their heads, it is on their feet. That they are turned downwards, is an obvious reference to their lives spent in gazing at the earth and earthly values, the earth as origin of wealth and material goods, of gold and silver, and now they will be confined within the object of their worldly desires. And there is a more particular reference in their punishment. The double repetition of St. Peter's name: "san Pietro" in *Inferno* xix.91 and "Pier" in line 94, may be compared to the two references to the word "pietra" in lines 14 and 75. This is an obvious reference to Christ's pun on *Petrus* and rock in the New Testament, the foundation of the Church on Peter, the rock. When we consider the fate of the predecessors of Nicholas who are interred in the fissures of the rock:

> per le fessure de la pietra piatti,   75

there is no question but that Dante represents these ecclesiastics as having mined gold and silver from the rock of the Church, indeed as having undermined the rock of Peter, and they are now punished by the reality of the honeycombed rock of Hell.[10] Because, although the moral indignation that inspires Dante in this canto comes from his horror at avarice, and, although the "maladetta lupa" looms in the background of *Inferno* xix as making the world miserable — he says of the popes:

> 'ché la vostra avarizia il mondo attrista,
> calcando i buoni e sollevando i pravi' —,   104-5

yet Dante's primary object is to condemn those who by their corruption or avarice are undermining the rock of the Church. His is an attack therefore on the Church in its persons. He refers to the Church as "la bella donna", betrayed by the adultery of her pastors (4), whose behaviour is described in these terms:

> Di voi pastor s'accorse il Vangelista,
>   quando colei che siede sopra l'acque
>   puttaneggiar coi regi a lui fu vista.   106-8

Later the Church is symbolized as "una puttana sciolta" (*Purg.*xxxii.149). Indeed the satire on the Church in the pageant in *Purgatorio* xxxii provides an appropriate clue to the emotion that prompts the dramatic unfolding of this canto when it is taken in conjunction with the close of *Inferno* xviii. The passage in *Purgatorio* xxxii reads:

> Sicura, quasi rocca in alto monte,
>   seder sovresso una puttana sciolta
>   m'apparve con le ciglia intorno pronte;
> e come perché non li fosse tolta,
>   vidi di costa a lei dritto un gigante;
>   e basciavansi insieme alcuna volta.
> Ma perché l'occhio cupido e vagante
>   a me rivolse, quel feroce drudo
>   la flagellò dal capo infin le piante;
> poi, di sospetto pieno e d'ira crudo,
>   disciolse il mostro, e trassel per la selva,
>   tanto che sol di lei mi fece scudo
> a la puttana e a la nova belva.   *Purg.*xxxii.148-60

This recalls the closing lines of *Inferno* xviii:

> Taïde è, la puttana che rispuose
>   al drudo suo quando disse 'Ho io grazie
>   grandi apo te?': 'Anzi maravigliose!'.   *Inf.*xviii.133-5

An atmosphere of sexual perversion and deceit was created by the description of the panders and seducers in *Inferno* xviii, in the references to Jason, who "Isifile ingannò" (*Inf.*xviii.92), to the "femmine da conio" (*Inf.*xviii.66), and continued with the explicit choice of Thais among the flatterers. This perversion is carried over into the reference in the opening lines of *Inferno* xix to adultery in the things of God; it recurs in the allusion to Boniface's deceit and exploitation:

> 'per lo qual non temesti tòrre a 'nganno
> la bella donna, e poi di farne strazio,'   56-7

and returns to the surface in the identification of the activity of the popes with that recorded in Revelation, "puttaneggiar coi regi" (108). It was Virgil who drew attention to the foul figure of Thais and alluded to her relationship as "puttana" with her "drudo", and Virgil will be exceptionally pleased with Dante's attack on the state of the Church:

> I' credo ben ch'al mio duca piacesse,
> con sí contenta labbia sempre attese
> lo suon de le parole vere espresse.   121-3

Thais, the "sozza e scapigliata fante" "con l'unghie merdose", is an appropriate image to introduce Dante's attack on the Church. The "puttana" answering her "drudo" so elliptically is reminiscent of the "puttana" casting "l'occhio cupido e vagante" (*Purg.*xxxii.154) on Dante in the earthly paradise and enraging her "drudo" there. Here Dante as he stares at the loathsome Thais seems prompted to recall the outrage of the Church taken by deceit and ravished. So that the puritanical outrage that led Dante to associate the contemporary Church with the whore of Babylon here and in *Purgatorio* xxxii is appropriately prompted by Thais and leads naturally to the drama and invective of *Inferno* xix.[11]

In fact Dante's emotion is shown straightaway in the early lines of *Inferno* xix by the slight incoherence in the opening address. This passage is characterized by a syntactical non sequitur, "e voi rapaci" (3) and by a profusion of relative clauses in lines 16-21. The disjointed syntax of the opening lines expresses Dante's alarm at the instability of the Church at the mercy of its rapacious pastors, the "lupi rapaci" of *Paradiso* xxvii.55. The emotion shown in this syntax throws suspicion on the seemingly *ex abrupto* beginning of the canto with the apostrophe to Simon Magus parallelled by the apostrophe to the "somma sapïenza" in line 10. This is the rhetoric of the narrative which seems to indicate the disembodied voice that is Dante remembering the event, writing about his experience, recovering the emotion and shock he suffered.[12]

But even if the content of *Inferno* xix may have been signalled by the emotional charge at the end of *Inferno* xviii and by some parallels in the two cantos, and even if parallels to its content are to be found throughout the *Commedia,* as a canto it stands solidly on its own.[13] Most of the canto is devoted to Dante's dialogue with Pope Nicholas III, who had died in 1280, and who reveals that in due course Boniface VIII will take his place, and that he in turn will be followed by a reputedly fouler simonist in the person of Clement V, who is to die in 1314. The remainder of the canto is taken up with Dante's attack on Nicholas and in general terms on the corruption of the Church and papacy and it concludes with Virgil's delighted bearing of Dante back up to the bridges over the Malebolge.

The structure of the canto falls into four distinct parts: lines 1-30 are introductory; in lines 31-87 Virgil and Dante descend to the rock-floor of the *bolgia* and seek out the great example of the sin,[14] Pope Nicholas III; lines 88-117 contain Dante's outburst of invective against simony in the Church and its corruption generally; in lines 118-33 Virgil and Dante ascend the side of the trench. These opening thirty lines introduce the cut and thrust, the surprises of the entire canto: a six-line apostrophe, a three-line narrative; a second apostrophe of three lines standing in contrast to the first; another three lines of narrative, followed by six lines that contain a nostalgic simile and a trenchant autobiographical anecdote. The opening six lines, the outburst against simonists, is followed at lines 10-12 by an approving outcry to divine justice which echoes part of the inscription over the entrance to Hell (*Inf*.iii.4-6), as Dante is reminded of heavenly things by the memory of the baseness of the sin of simony and the subterranean nature of its punishment. Six lines (13-18), describe the place of their confinement and then the sinners themselves are described (22-30) as protruding their legs with the soles of the feet aflame.[15]

Dante's way of introducing the canto is another example of his command of dramatic effect. This is the first time at the beginning of a canto that Dante introduces the narrative with an apostrophe. With this address, Dante recalls the experience, evokes in memory the presence of Simon Magus underground. The play on *Simon/simoneggiando* (74) recalls Simon Peter as well as Simon the simonist to stress the antithesis that underlies the entire episode, the antithesis of the sound Church and the undermined. He heralds the condemnation of Church and popes with "suoni la tromba" (5). This trumpeting in the opening lines, heard in the onomatopoeic resonance of the early passages as far as line 21,[16] is an ominous introduction to the theme of the canto and also expresses the fierce satisfaction that he felt in contemplating the punishment-to-be of his enemy Boniface.

From the address to the individual Simon Magus, Dante's condemnation switches to the "voi rapaci" of churchmen and simonists, an alternation between an individual and a collective "voi" that is to occur later in the canto in the condemnation of the individual popes and of the collective papacy (104-11). These early lines culminate in what seems to be an attempt to avoid censure for his later invective against the Church by the autobiographical anecdote which casts him in the role of protagonist in an event somehow reminiscent of the role he is about to play here.

> Non mi parean men ampi né maggiori
> che que' che son nel mio bel San Giovanni,
> fatti per loco d'i battezzatori;
> l'un de li quali, ancor non è molt' anni,
> rupp' io per un che dentro v'annegava:
> e questo sia suggel ch'ogn' omo sganni.   16-21

The grouping of the words "nel mio bel San Giovanni" focuses in a way understandable to every reader, the "carità del natio loco" (*Inf.*xiv.1). It is only one of the many places where Dante in exile expresses nostalgia for a city that had expelled him. The longing for his birthplace prepares his dramatic attack on Boniface and, by recalling the poignant memories of the exile, paves the way for his anger and resentment against the Pope as a cause of his exile. Possibly, too, as well as explaining it, the image and memory also motivate the attack. Although it is possible to interpret these lines without ascribing nostalgia to them, nostalgia is clearly present later in the *Commedia,* when he puts his hope in this "poema sacro" that he is composing, to overcome the cruelty that has closed him out of the "bello ovile ov' io dormi' agnello" where he dwelt securely, a lamb within the fold, as a boy, and where he hopes he will return as poet (*Par.*xxv.1-9)

> . . . e in sul fonte
> del mio battesmo prenderò 'l cappello,

to be crowned with laurel in the Baptistery at the font where he was baptized.

The most straight-forward explanation of the line,

> e questo sia suggel ch'ogn' omo sganni,   21

in relation to the autobiographical anecdote, is that Dante here clears up any difficulties in understanding what exactly happened on that occasion. This is the best interpretation,

because it makes sense. Any other interpretation begs a
question, or twists the text, or seems far-fetched. But often
Dante's clear statements have become opaque on examination.
For example, it has been said that Dante here is claiming
authorship of his poem, in case it should be disputed. But as the
evidence for his authorship is legion throughout the poem, in
his account of associates, his relationship with Florence, with
Beatrice, this is hardly a tenable solution.[17] Again it is said that
as he was an exile, at the mercy of all kinds of accusations, so
here he is answering a charge of sacrilege in breaking the holy
font. But in exile from Florence he was sentenced for
corruption in public life but never seemingly accused of
sacrilege. Of early commentators on the poem one claims to
have seen a broken font, another states that a boy, whose name
is given, was playing near the font and fell in, and that Dante
released him. A more far-reaching and beguiling approach, is
that of the parable explanation: an event from the personal life
of Dante expresses symbolically the meaning of the present
canto: "Dante's breaking the stone font to save a human life" is
an image of the "breaking" of the corrupt and undermined rock
of the papacy that oppresses man's spiritual life, the figurative
breaking that Dante executes in this canto. Overall, the best
implication is that as the earlier act of freeing someone was free
from irreverence, so now the attack on the popes he is about to
launch is "equally free from irreverence".[18]

These lines on San Giovanni and its font and Dante's
anecdote, have firstly the force of nostalgia, justifying in
dramatic or poetic terms at least, his attack on Boniface for
causing his exile; secondly, they offer what may be
reconstructed as a visual anticipation of the sight he now
presents in the next lines of the waving legs as he looks at the
floor of Hell. Thirdly, he then, as now, acted according to the
dictates of what was necessary, no more, no less.

The slight confusion and obscurity of the opening part of
Inferno xix prefigure in condensed form what follows in the
canto. The syntactical non sequitur of singular and plural in

the opening lines, the profusion of relative clauses, the confusion over the reference in the anecdote, the emphatic but sibylline line 21, the emotion he feels at the perversion of the Church and the iron in his soul because of exile, all of these, from the evocation of Simon Magus to the memory of waving legs, present in fragmented form a preliminary dumb-show of the scene and harangue that are to follow.

Of the first thirty lines only twelve are indispensable for the narrative:

> Già eravamo, a la seguente tomba,
>   montati de lo scoglio in quella parte
>   ch'a punto sovra mezzo 'l fosso piomba.   7-9

> Io vidi per le coste e per lo fondo
>   piena la pietra livida di fóri,
>   d'un largo tutti e ciascun era tondo.   13-15

> Fuor de la bocca a ciascun soperchiava
>   d'un peccator li piedi e de le gambe
>   infino al grosso, e l'altro dentro stava.
> Le piante erano a tutti accese intrambe;
>   per che sí forte guizzavan le giunte,
>   che spezzate averien ritorte e strambe.   22-7

As far as line 30 everything is matter-of-fact in the narrative, to maintain the illusion of fact, indeed the spare narration in these lines is deliberate, merely as attention is focused on the two apostrophes, and the autobiographical anecdote. But that supposedly factual picture before the eyes is a strange one, and now it becomes the basis for what may be called the *divertimento* of dancing legs that Dante has prepared. If the dance and the dancers are at first sight described in unremarkable, straightforward terms, he goes on in the encounter with the pope to elaborate his use of the grotesque, a grotesque that is acceptable as a result of the sober presentation of the scene.

At line 31, the second section opens with the innocent-seeming question:

> 'Chi è colui, maestro, che si cruccia
>   guizzando piú che li altri suoi consorti',
>   diss' io, 'e cui piú roggia fiamma succia?'   31-3

Here Dante identifies the one who will best fulfil his desire for satisfaction. The game begins, first with the false naiveté, the innocent question, where with sophisticated malice, the author has himself as character pick out unerringly the chief amongst them. By means of the convention where the important person in a painting is bigger than lesser companions, or wears more distinctive clothing, Dante, in a variant of this convention, reviews that mass of legs and has his attention drawn to the pair of legs that kicks harder than any other and is burned by a flame redder than any of the others. The feet are not just burned, the word used is "succia", and it is hard to deny that "succia" is onomatopoeic. Dante introduces the note of gesture, of expression, to the legs. Here the legs of the pope express the sufferer's torment: "si cruccia". Later with his leg, the spirit weeps in line 45, and in line 64, he "wrings" or twists his feet in dejection, and finally in line 120 he expresses, either because of anger or the bite of his conscience, his strength of feeling in his kicking. These four touches of the grotesque mime are placed strategically along the way of the canto to induce an overall acquiescence in this most incredible of encounters, a willed suspension of disbelief, willed by the writer, unconscious in the reader. Dante enables us to accept the impossible.

To Dante's question Virgil does not offer an answer, rather knowing what is in store, he offers to carry Dante down the side of the trench to ask the spirit directly about himself and his sins.[19] Then Dante shows his complete trust in Virgil in his reply:

'tu se' segnore, e sai ch'i' non mi parto
dal tuo volere, e sai quel che si tace.'   38-9

This seems to indicate that Virgil knows Dante's unspoken
thoughts and wishes and it anticipates further what is to come.

They have now crossed the third *bolgia* and on the lower side
of this third of nine concentric trenches that descend into
the inverted cone of lower Hell, Virgil, turning left, bears
Dante down into the pit. He carries him as far as the individual
Dante had asked about:

Allor venimmo in su l'argine quarto;
    volgemmo e discendemmo a mano stanca
    là giú nel fondo foracchiato e arto.
Lo buon maestro ancor de la sua anca
    non mi dipuose, sí mi giunse al rotto
    di quel che si piangeva con la zanca.   40-5

Dante, again with seeming innocence, addresses this
unidentified figure:

'O qual che se' che 'l di sú tien di sotto,
    anima trista come pal commessa',
    comincia' io a dir, 'se puoi, fa motto'.   46-8

In this he implies that he hardly expects the grotesque posture
of the sinner to allow him to speak. But if that is his expect-
ation in the simile that follows, by recording speech from the
assassin set alive in the burial position head well below ground,
he prepares the reader to expect speech from the similarly
positioned pope:

Io stava come 'l frate che confessa
    lo perfido assessin, che, poi ch'è fitto,
    richiama lui per che la morte cessa.   49-51

This is one of those complex similes, that admit analysis but defy invention, and remain to fill the imagination with specific images, answering unspoken needs in the narrative, averting possible doubts and preparing the reader for what is to come, reinforcing previous effects, colouring the emotions and, in this case, interchanging dramatically and with deliberate intent priest and layman. The effect then is to give us a visual picture of Dante listening to a head-down figure. This is ostensibly the only purpose of the simile, but there is also the moral judgment conveyed by Dante's identification of himself with the priest and the pope with the assassin, and in one of those strokes of invention that characterize his writing, the addition of "perfido" to "assessin" damns by inference the pope, who is beneath him. A primary function of the simile is to provide an answer to any doubt about the ability of this "anima trista" to speak from that position. If the assassin set head down in the ground can speak to his confessor, it never occurs to us to doubt or even question the mechanics of voice reproduction by the legs that turn out to be those of a pope.

For this is Nicholas III who was one of the Orsini as his own epigrammatic words, with the bitter gibe about his nepotism, show:

> 'e veramente fui figliuol de l'orsa,
>   cupido sí per avanzar li orsatti,
>   che sú l'avere e qui me misi in borsa.'   70-2

He was pope from 1277 to 1280 and his period in power is not one that historians have found very important or worthy of exceptional study. Some commentators, especially in the nineteenth century, claim that Dante was wrong to put in Hell such a holy man, whose only fault was that he was over-zealous in advancing his own relations. However among Dante's contemporaries this was seen as a serious fault. The most comprehensive early account is given by Villani,who says that when Nicholas was a young cleric and later cardinal, "fu onestissimo e di buona vita", but when he became pope he changed; he advanced favourites and, says Villani in a phrase that explains, or at least supports and corroborates Dante's selection of Nicholas as his great example of the sin, "fu de' primi o il primo papa nella cui corte s'usasse palese simonia per li suoi parenti."[20] This explains the intensity of the self-accusation of Nicholas.

The immediate reaction to Dante's question is the recognition scene which is a mistaken recognition as neither time nor person is right. Nicholas cries: "se' tu già costí ritto, Bonifazio?" (53). This so stuns Dante that Virgil has to intervene quickly to prevent the misunderstanding from going any further, forcefully telling Dante to deny that he is Boniface and to deny that Boniface has come. Ironically Nicholas thinks Dante of all people is Boniface: a startling and dramatic error, especially for Dante the character. Nicholas's amazement and emotion comes in the repetition of one group of words twice and of "se' tu" three times:

> Ed el gridò: 'Se' tu già costí ritto,
> se' tu già costí ritto, Bonifazio?
> Di parecchi anni mi mentí lo scritto.
> Se' tu sí tosto di quell' aver sazio
> per lo qual non temesti tòrre a 'nganno
> la bella donna, e poi di farne strazio?'   52-7

It is hardly too much to read sarcasm into that repeated "ritto",the knowledge that Boniface is enjoying his last moments of being upright. But that is the deeper irony; the more obvious one, as has been pointed out, is that Nicholas, to Dante's bewilderment mistakes him for Boniface, Dante's great enemy. In Dante's Hell, the damned can dimly foresee the future but present events are shrouded, as Farinata said:

> 'Noi veggiam, come quei c'ha mala luce,
> le cose', disse, 'che ne son lontano;

cotanto ancor ne splende il sommo duce.
Quando s'appressano o son, tutto è vano
   nostro intelletto; e s'altri non ci apporta,
   nulla sapem di vostro stato umano.'   *Inf.*x.100-5

This is the cause of Nicholas III's amazement. His blindness to
contemporary events in the world and his awareness of
Boniface's expected death in 1303, lead to his confusion. But
more obvious still is the prophetic irony, that Boniface is
named as the next to come to that tormented pass. Dante's
reaction is one of bewilderment given in another simile of the
type characterized by C.S. Lewis as Dante's favourite type of
simile, comparing an emotion with an emotion:[21]

Tal mi fec' io, quai son color che stanno,
   per non intender ciò ch'è lor risposto,
   quasi scornati, e risponder non sanno.   58-60

For a moment Dante as character is placed in the position of
one who has not grasped the significance of a particular joke,
one who suspects he is being tricked, unaware of what the true
situation is, in common with the unfortunate prelate beneath
him. Only Virgil can reassure Dante with the repeated "non son
colui" (62-3). Dante here is making use of a device to control
the reader, pretending that he knew nothing of all this, but in
fact damning for all time his enemy Boniface. Dramatically,
then, he is innocent of the punishment of Boniface.

The reaction from this fiendish piece of dramatic irony then
sets in. Nicholas III, after the surprise and Dante's denial,
shows dejection, then asks and answers his own question:

. . . 'Dunque che a me richiedi?
Se di saper ch'i' sia ti cal cotanto,
   che tu abbi però la ripa corsa,
   sappi ch'i' fui vestito del gran manto.'   66-9

The Pope identifies himself in a speech from lines 67-87, in
concise and telling language, acknowledging his sin in a bitter
epigram:

> che sú l'avere e qui me misi in borsa. 72

He describes the fate of his predecessors who have descended
beneath his head into the fissures of the rock:

> Di sotto al capo mio son li altri tratti
> che precedetter me simoneggiando,
> per le fessure de la pietra piatti. 73-5

He prophesies the coming of Boniface VIII, whose arrival he
had already dramatically presented when he mistook Dante for
him:

> Là giú cascherò io altresí quando
> verrà colui ch'i' credea che tu fossi,
> allor ch'i' feci 'l súbito dimando. 76-8

He then foretells that Clement V will replace Boniface in his
turn:

> ché dopo lui verrà di piú laida opra,
> di ver' ponente, un pastor sanza legge,
> tal che convien che lui e me ricuopra. 82-4

The epigrammatical nature of the speech of Nicholas
demonstrates the concentrated bitterness of the pope's
personality, and it is a good example of the compression of
Dante's style. The line,

> 'sappi ch'i' fui vestito del gran manto,' 69

with the metonymy of the "gran manto" standing for the
papacy, later to be repeated by Adrian V:

'Un mese e poco piú prova' io come
   pesa il gran manto a chi dal fango il guarda,
   che piuma sembran tutte l'altre some,' *Purg.*xix.103-5

leads to "e veramente fui figliuol de l'orsa" (70). Nicholas
identifies himself as one of the Orsini family who signed
themselves on official contemporary documents in Latin as of
the sons of the bear, *de filiis Ursae*, so that Dante is exact here.
Also he puns on the proverbial or supposed nature of the bear
and Nicholas bitterly draws our attention to the pun by
saying "veramente" "truly I was a son of the bear, not just an
Orsini", but also an imitator of the nature of the bear. The bear
is said to be gluttonous and jealously dedicated to its offspring,
in this case the "orsatti" of the following line.[22] Here "cupido"
also applies to the character of Nicholas and to the nature of
the sin, as Dante relates simony to "cupidigia" or "avarizia". As
said before, line 72 gives in a nutshell the sin and the style: "che
sú l'avere e qui me misi in borsa". Again, this is a pun that
reinforces the earlier play on Simon Magus and Simon Peter
and also the *Pietro/pietra* pun, for in "Malebolge", "bolgia",
mentioned here in line 6, has a double meaning: ditch or pouch.
Of himself Nicholas crushingly repeats the word "avere" he
used to Boniface, as he then supposed, in line 55:

'Se' tu sí tosto di quell' aver sazio',

to say that he pouched material possessions in his life and here
is pouched himself.
   It is interesting to note that Nicholas is not derogatory
merely about his own behaviour as a simonist, but he attacks
Boniface quite savagely with that power of compressed
rhetoric and skill in expression with which Dante endows him.
Boniface VIII is here, in the words of Nicholas, described as the
ravager of the "bella donna" in line 57, that is: he who
prostitutes the Church, having espoused her; he who obtained
the papacy by deceit; and, condensed in the same three lines, is

the previouly mentioned accusation of interest in material
possessions and of having more than his fill of them. This
attack on Boniface is followed by the attack on Clement V:

> 'Nuovo Iasón sarà, di cui si legge
> ne' Maccabei; e come a quel fu molle
> suo re, cosí fia lui chi Francia regge.'   85-7

This was the first pope of the so-called Babylonian captivity of
the popes, who set up the papal court in Avignon in 1309.
Villani once again supports Dante's interpretation: "fu uomo
molto cupido di moneta e simoniaco", and each of these words
is applied to a pope in this canto. Dante refers to him with
deep contempt, but without the personal antipathy that he feels
for Boniface, yet on the evidence here: "di piú laida opra" (82),
"un pastor sanza legge" (83), he would seem to consider him to
be worse than his great enemy. This surprising judgment is
masked by the rhetorical structure of Nicholas's speech.[23]

The climax of the speech with its reference to the Old
Testament Jason[24] and its progression from the sins of
Nicholas and a recollection of the sins of Boniface already
revealed, to the deep ignominy for the Church with the papacy
of Clement, gives Dante the opportunity of launching upon
one of the most unrestrained invectives in the *Divina
Commedia* from his own mouth. With an initial disclaimer:

> Io non so s'i' mi fui qui troppo folle,   88

Dante recounts two thirds of the way through the canto how he
inveighed first against Nicholas himself, then against simonists
in general, but particularly popes guilty of simony, and finally
against the Church. This speech runs from line 88 to 117. As
Nicholas had effectively prophesied first the death of Boniface,
to take place in 1303, three and a half years after the date at
which Dante's vision is set, and then the pontificate and death
of Clement from 1305 to 1314, Dante takes the opportunity of

reviling the contemporary papacy. He first rebuts the reference
to scripture with two texts that place simony in perspective:

> ' . . . quanto tesoro volle
> Nostro Segnore in prima da san Pietro
>   ch'ei ponesse le chiavi in sua balía?
> Certo non chiese se non "Viemmi retro".
> Né Pier né li altri tolsero a Matia
>   oro od argento, quando fu sortito
>   al loco che perdé l'anima ria.'   90-6

He then deals with the exemplary nature of the just punishment
of Nicholas:

> 'Però ti sta, ché tu se' ben punito'.   97

While upbraiding Nicholas he makes the transition from the
individual to the general by enlarging the particular
condemnation to include the many indicated by the use of
"vostra" in the judgment pronounced at lines 104-5. The whole
passage which includes criticism of Nicholas III and a possibly
apocryphal gibe about his relationship with Charles of Anjou
reads:[25]

> 'Però ti sta, ché tu se' ben punito;
>   e guarda ben la mal tolta moneta
>   ch'esser ti fece contra Carlo ardito.
> E se non fosse ch'ancor lo mi vieta
>   la reverenza de le somme chiavi
>   che tu tenesti ne la vita lieta,
> io userei parole ancor piú gravi;
>   ché la vostra avarizia il mondo attrista,
>   calcando i buoni e sollevando i pravi.'   97-105

This leads naturally and coherently to his review of the state of
the Church at the close of his speech, for he goes on to adopt an

apocalyptic, biblical tone in his polemical condemnation of the prelates and pontiffs of the Church:[26]

'Di voi pastor s'accorse il Vangelista,
  quando colei che siede sopra l'acque
  puttaneggiar coi regi a lui fu vista;
quella che con le sette teste nacque,
  e da le diece corna ebbe argomento,
  fin che virtute al suo marito piacque.
Fatto v'avete dio d'oro e d'argento;
  e che altro è da voi a l'idolatre,
  se non ch'elli uno, e voi ne orate cento?'   106-14

Thus in fiercely oratorical style he first attacks Nicholas from line 90 to 103, using the "tu" form, then from line 104 to 117, using "voi", he broadens the scope of his attack to include the Church as a whole.

Those lines 106-11 express Dante's views in Revelation terms.[27] He concludes his speech with the third apostrophe in the canto, "Ahi Costantin", that in vocabulary and imagery sums up his attitude to simony as well as to the Church and, beneath the three lines of this highly-coloured, rhetorical address that condemns the gift of temporal possessions but not the giver,[28] Dante expands his criticism of the Church in historical terms:

'Ahi, Costantin, di quanto mal fu matre,
  non la tua conversion, ma quella dote
  che da te prese il primo ricco patre!'   115-17

After the address to "Simon mago", after the call on heavenly wisdom "O somma sapïenza", the third address proper in the canto to an absent person or personification occurs here. This is a sad one, showing Dante's despondency at the ill-effects of the famous Donation which the fourth-century Emperor Constantine at the time of his conversion was supposed to have

made to Pope Sylvester when he handed over to the Roman
Pontiff political power over the West. The Donation is a ninth-
century forgery but Dante did not know this and he thought it
the most disastrous political error ever committed as it
confused the temporal and spiritual power of the pope.[29] His
indictment of the popes is thus set in historical perspective by
this regretful closure to the speech. It also marks Dante's
political position as intransigent. The only successful reform of
the Church that he could envisage would mean a reversal of the
historical process that had been started by the Donation and a
return of the Church to an exclusive interest in spiritual power.
This radical position made Dante politically an anticlerical,
and the final words of this violently anticlerical speech, the
bitter irony of describing Sylvester I as "il primo ricco patre",
juxtaposed with a "matre" of "mal", emphasize his
uncompromising attitude to what he saw as corruption that
had to be extirpated.

The last section describes the reaction of the legs
addressed:[30]

> E mentr' io li cantava cotai note,
>   o ira o cosc'ienza che 'l mordesse,
>   forte spingava con ambo le piote.   118-20

This is the last touch in Dante's portrayal of the personality of
Nicholas, a character than whom Foster says there are greater
in the *Inferno,* "but none more vividly presented than this
fretful, sharp-tongued, irascible priest - who is presented, let us
remember only through his voice, he is never *seen.*"[31] But now
the hidden voice is stilled and only the legs are eloquent and
reflect the force of Dante's condemnation.

Dante expresses his satisfaction at his own personal
performance by describing Virgil's approval:

> I' credo ben ch'al mio duca piacesse,
>   con sí contenta labbia sempre attese

lo suon de le parole vere espresse.
Però con ambo le braccia mi prese;
e poi che tutto su mi s'ebbe al petto,
rimontò per la via onde discese.   121-6

Dante has no misgivings here, indeed, Virgil's approval recalls his outspoken approval of a previous intervention by Dante. When in *Inferno* viii Dante vilified Filippo Argenti, Virgil embraced him:

Lo collo poi con le braccia mi cinse;
basciommi 'l volto e disse: 'Alma sdegnosa,
benedetta colei che 'n te s'incinse!'   *Inf.*viii.43-5

Here once again, Virgil, well-pleased, gathers Dante to himself, bears him up the side and over the edge on to the bridge that runs over the next trench. Dante ends the canto when Virgil sets him down "soavemente" on the rough surface and he prepares calmly for the next stage of his journey:

Indi un altro vallon mi fu scoperto.   133

In the desire to relate the various implications of Dante's attitude to the simonists and his treatment of them, efforts have been made to equate their upturned legs with the upturned legs of Lucifer,[32] which Dante is to see when he passes the pit of Hell, imagined as the centre of the world. Lucifer is an enormous almost immobile caricature of hate, a crowning grotesque for the grotesque experiences of Hell, wedged in the centre of the earth, and when Dante passes through that centre and looks back he sees these monstrous legs stretching up. This is not a convincing identification chiefly because Lucifer's legs are held immobile,[33] and those of the simonists are not. A more obvious correspondence is with Judas. At *Inferno* xix.96, when Dante says that Matthias took the place of the "anima ria", he means Judas, and the passage in the Acts on the election of

Matthias has Peter describe the death of Judas. Judas betrayed for money; as with Simon Magus,[34] silver was his idea of a reward; and the "mal tolta moneta" in line 98 so hard upon the "anima ria" in line 96 is intended to cause an identification between the simoniacal pope and the traitor to Christ.

As "somme chiavi" here, and "gran manto" here and in *Purgatorio* xix stand for the papacy, "pietra" stands for the Church: a rock riddled by parasites to such an extent that when Lucifer is described as the "vermo reo che 'l mondo fóra" (*Inf.*xxxiv.108), the comparison is inevitable. As the popes do to the Church, Lucifer does to the world. This leads naturally to the identification of the popes with Judas, Lucifer with Antichrist; and Dante never identifies Boniface with Antichrist.[35] When Dante comes close later to Lucifer, he finds there three faces: and in the mouths of Satan he sees on either side the protruding heads of the two traitors of the Empire, Brutus and Cassius, but pride of place in human terms in the *Inferno* goes to the dangling legs of Judas from the central mouth, great traitor of the Church,

> 'che 'l capo ha dentro e fuor le gambe mena.'
>
> (*Inf.*xxxiv.63)

This is a far more likely identification than that with Lucifer himself. Indeed Lucifer's legs form a stiff contrast to the legs in the canto. But the legs of Judas dangling from the mouth of Lucifer in *Inferno* xxxiv are evocative of those in *Inferno* xix. These are legs that can be seen to this day in the vault of Dante's "bel San Giovanni" dangling from the mouth of the enthroned Lucifer, although it is not certain that Dante saw those mosaics.

In *Inferno* xix Dante shows his emotional and intellectual repudiation of the contemporary Church. He presents popes as successors of Simon Magus as opposed to Simon Peter and, to complete the antithesis, he identifies their activity since the Donation of Constantine with the undermining of the rock of

Peter and not with building on its foundations. He suggests an identification with Judas but not with the devil and not with Antichrist.

As has been pointed out, Dante is intent in *Inferno* xix on describing an anti-Church as the reality in Hell of the contemporary Church on earth. This is brought out by means of the contrasting ideals that St. Peter sets out in Heaven. After his prologue (*Par.*xxvii.22-7), which has already been quoted at the beginning of this commentary, St. Peter goes on to pronounce:

> 'Non fu la sposa di Cristo allevata
>   del sangue mio, di Lin, di quel di Cleto,
>   per essere ad acquisto d'oro usata;
> ma per acquisto d'esto viver lieto
>   e Sisto e Pïo e Calisto e Urbano
>   sparser lo sangue dopo molto fleto.
> Non fu nostra intenzion ch'a destra mano
>   d'i nostri successor parte sedesse,
>   parte da l'altra del popol cristiano;
> né che le chiavi che mi fuor concesse,
>   divenisser signaculo in vessillo
>   che contra battezzati combattesse;
> né ch'io fossi figura di sigillo
>   a privilegi venduti e mendaci,
>   ond' io sovente arrosso e disfavillo.
> In vesta di pastor lupi rapaci
>   si veggion di qua sú per tutti i paschi:
>   o difesa di Dio, perché pur giaci?
> Del sangue nostro Caorsini e Guaschi
>   s'apparecchian di bere: o buon principio,
>   a che vil fine convien che tu caschi!'   *Par.*xxvii.40-60

However, help will soon be at hand and in the following lines Peter, invoking the intervention of Providence, seems to suggest that Dante's poem should play its part in salvation (*Par.*xxvii.61-6).

It is in this context that Dante's outspoken condemnation of the Church and churchmen should be understood. With the "imprimatur" of St. Peter, he casts himself as judge, never more so than in this canto. And he prepares for the role specifically in the canto by recalling the episode from his life in which, driven by whatever necessity, he intervened in church. Whatever about the exact meaning of the Baptistery anecdote, it seems clear that Dante uses it in context to amplify his description and to give a local focus to the scene described and to the far-reaching implications of the episode that is to follow. And it may be further argued that in this canto the tension between Dante author and Dante character is momentarily exacerbated by the very fact that Dante is satisfying what is evidently a deeply felt desire to damn Boniface. He therefore uses this autobiographical anecdote to cast himself in an exemplary role, to justify what might otherwise be considered self-indulgence. Moreover, motivated by artistic concern, he no doubt wishes to distract attention from what might be an exaggeratedly personal intrusion, were it not balanced by the corresponding strength in the real life story.

Dante's particular disgust at the state of the Church is reflected by his use of perverted sexual imagery which, though largely conventional within the bounds of the canto itself, assumes greater emotional force when it is seen to be related to the terms and descriptions of the previous canto and of *Purgatorio* xxxii. His root and branch criticism of the contemporary Church much pleased his mentor Virgil and marks a major step in the character development of self within the poem.[36]

But the enduring memory of the canto is its association with comedy. The comedy appears in the bizarre shock of Dante finding himself identified as his great enemy, so that a momentary, tongue-tied crisis of identity occurs, as the realization dawns that he has succeeded in damning Boniface to Hell. And over all remain the cruel, grotesque *divertimento* or dancing of legs and the peevish eloquence of Nicholas whose expression is given added richness by the miming of his legs that weep or sigh, and wring their feet in distress, and kick with temper as the poet fulminates.

Notes

[1]St. Peter says:

> 'e tu figliuol, che per lo mortal pondo
>   ancor giú tornerai, apri la bocca,
>   e non asconder quel ch'io non ascondo.' *Par.*xxvii.64-6

In *Purgatorio* xxxii Beatrice had said:

> 'Però, in pro del mondo che mal vive,
>   al carro tieni or li occhi, e quel che vedi,
>   ritornato di là, fa che tu scrive.'   *Purg.*xxxii.103-5

[2]The most important readings of this canto in recent years have been: J. A. Scott, "The Rock of Peter and *Inferno* XIX", *Romance Philology,* 23 (1970), 462-79; M. Musa, "Aesthetic Structure in the *Inferno, Canto XIX*" in *Essays on Dante,* ed. M. Musa (Bloomington, 1964); and again in M. Musa, "From Measurement to Meaning: Simony", *Advent at the Gates* (Bloomington, 1974) pp. 37-64; K. Foster, "The Canto of the Damned Popes:*Inferno* XIX", *Dante Studies,* 87 (1969), 47-68; P. Brezzi, "*Inferno* XIX", *Nuove letture dantesche,* Volume II (Florence, 1968), pp. 161-82; A. Pagliaro, *Il canto XIX dell'Inferno,* Lectura Dantis Scaligera (Florence, 1961) and in his *Ulisse:Ricerche semantiche sulla Divina Commedia,* 2 vols (Messina, 1966), II, 253-309; E. Sanguineti, *Interpretazione di Malebolge* (Florence, 1961). See also F. D'Ovidio, "Il canto

XIX dell'Inferno", *Letture dantesche:Inferno,* ed. G. Getto, Volume I (Florence, 1955), pp. 345-76, reprinted with omissions from his "Il canto dei simoniaci" in *Nuovi studi danteschi* (Milan, 1907), pp. 337-443, also referred to as *Ugolino, Pier della Vigna, i simoniaci.*

[3]That Pope Adrian V is encountered in *Purgatorio* xix is in itself an obvious parallel with the popes in *Inferno* xix. Apart from the line:

> *scias quod ego fui successor Petri,*   Purg.xix.99

there is also the deliberate echo in the use of the same metonymy , "gran manto", both by Adrian and Nicholas III. For a discussion of Adrian, see Scott, pp. 465-6 and 469-70. See also Foster, p. 55.

[4]J. Rivière, *Le problème de l'église et de l'état au temps de Philippe le Bel* (Paris, 1926) in the extract translated by C. T. Wood, pp. 66-70 of *Philip the Fair and Boniface VIII: State Vs. Papacy,* European Problem Studies, ed. C. T. Wood (New York, 1967), p. 68. Rivière saw Boniface as a conservative in his doctrine.

[5]G. Villani, *Cronica,* VIII, 5-6; Foster, pp. 55 and 66-7. See also C. T. Wood, p. 76 note 4 above.

[6]Most of the quotations from Villani are drawn from *Cronica,* VII and VIII, and are given by all the standard commentators. See C. T. Wood, p. 22.

[7]Acts, 8: 14-24.

[8]Domenico Palmieri, *Commento alla Divina Commedia di Dante Alighieri,* 3 vols (Prato, 1898), I, p. 377, says: "A' seduttori, i quali per interesse, ... si cattivano l'amor della donna ed agli adulatori, tengono dietro coloro che per interesse fanno l'invaghito della Chiesa e delle cose sante di Dio. Le cose di Dio denno essere spose di bontà, cioè sposate alla virtù e al merito di chi le ottiene, non all'animo turpe che agogna il danaro: il simoniaco le adultera, sposandole al vizio, le prostituisce e ciò per amor dell'oro e dell'argento, ed egli stesso

è quindi adultero, non legittimo sposo della Chiesa, cui prende nelle sue braccia (i vescovi diconsi sposi della loro Chiesa): tutti sono rapaci, e, secondo l'Alighieri, frodolenti; poichè siamo in Malebolge. Ma dove sta il vizio della frode? Nel contratto simoniaco, tra i due contraenti non corre frode; chè ciascuno sa quel che vuole, quel che si compra e quello che si sborsa. La frode è fatta alla Chiesa, che viene ingannata, dandole lupi sotto sembianza di pastori. Forse perchè il simoniaco perverte l'ordine, facendo servire lo spirituale al temporale, i simoniaci sono puniti collo stare capovolti e perchè mettono danari in borsa e ve li stivano, qui sono chiusi e serrati in uno stretto buco."

[9]Foster, p. 64, notes how Dante, "while ringing the changes on terms denoting money and material possessions, returns with a certain persistence to the same expression, 'gold and silver'. This expression is taken from the Bible and its repetition — it occurs three times — is a factor in the markedly biblical flavour of the canto as a whole. The Simoniacs, in the opening cry, are those who prostitute sacred things 'per oro e per argento', which, fifty verses on, in the first thrust at Boniface VIII (v. 55), become 'aver', possessions, and this word is repeated in verse 72, in the concrete sense of money kept in a purse. Then, in the first half of Dante's final speech, we get the three synonyms, 'treasure', 'gold and silver', and lastly the clinching term 'money', 'moneta'. The chief biblical texts so far recalled are, in the first place, Our Lord's charge to the Apostles (Matthew 10:8-9 and parallels): 'Freely have you received, freely give. Take no gold or silver or copper in your purses'; and then Peter's answer to the beggar at the Temple gate in Acts 3:6: 'Silver and gold I have none, but what I have I give you: in the name of Jesus of Nazareth, get up and walk'. But when the phrase is used for the third time, associating avarice with idolatry (v. 112), the echoes come rather from the Old Testament, from the Psalms and Isaiah and Hosea, from all that ancient polemic against idolatry which Christianity sanctioned and presupposed; but most directly no doubt from

the words of Hosea: 'Of their silver and gold they have made idols' (8:4)."

[10]Scott, p. 464, was the first to note and develop "the striking parallel set up by the poet between the rock of Hell and the rock of Peter, which pervades the whole canto ", and he interprets the anecdote of Dante's breaking the baptismal font to accord with his action in the present canto where "to save the world from total ruin, the Church and its spiritual head must be liberated from the *pietra* of greed in which they are buried and suffocating to death" (p. 477).

[11]Musa noted the relevance of Thais but does not mention the passage from *Purgatorio* xxxii; he is satisfied with the casual biblical image of "puttaneggiar" (*Inf.*xix.108) as an echo of "puttana" (*Inf.*xviii.133). Foster finds lines 106-8 in *Inferno* xix rather forced, "the only infelicity I find in this speech" (p. 61). Taken in conjunction with *Purgatorio* xxxii, Musa's argument for a correspondence is, I believe, proven. There are other correspondences between *Inferno* xviii and xix that are worth noting at least in a general way. The "inganno" attributed to Boniface (*Inf.*xix.56) echoes the threefold "ingannò", "ingannate", "inganna" (*Inf.*xviii.92-7), and the panders and seducers in *Inferno* xviii are likened to the crowds summoned to Rome by Boniface in 1300 for "l'anno del giubileo" (*Inf.*xviii.28-33); the perversion of the image of adultery of holy things for gold and silver in the opening lines of *Inferno* xix recalls the "femmine da conio" in *Inf.*xviii.66; again, the occurrence of Jason the Argonaut in *Inferno* xviii and the Old Testament Jason the priest in *Inferno* xix is possibly intended and must have been noticed by Dante, and the final phrase of *Inferno* xviii

'e quinci sian le nostre viste sazie'   136

may also find a corresponding echo in *Inferno* xix.55:

'se' tu sí tosto di quell' aver sazio?'

Whether Dante genuinely or deliberately misunderstood Cicero, *De Amicitia* and Terence, *Eunuchus* II, i; or whether, as Casini notes, he is thinking of *Eunuchus* III, ii, or giving a dramatic rendering of the courtesan, are unresolved questions. But what emerges from the filth of the second trench of Malebolge is an episode in which sexuality and flattery are inextricably combined. (Of the commentators the one who responds most to the sexuality of Thais is Momigliano). For, led by Cicero, Dante seeks out Terence for a flatterer and finds in *Eunuchus* III, ii, 4-5 the dialogue between Thais and her "drudo" in which at one point she answers "plurimum, merito tuo". This is recalled here just before the evocation in *Inferno* xix.1 of Simon Magus, who in *Paradiso* xxx.146 is said to be "per suo merto" in Hell. It seems likely then that the image of Thais as a "puttana" specifically in the relation to her "drudo", coupled with the loathsome description of her as courtesan, releases the emotion of disgust which Dante seems to feel, puritanically and paternalistically, in his indictment of the Church in *Inferno* xix. Having said as much, it is important to apply any such judgment with caution, not to say tact, to a work so rich in implications as the *Divina Commedia*.

[12]As we learn from the closing lines of *Paradiso* xxx, Simon Magus is in fact in the circle of the simonists, within the rock, although Dante in *Inferno* xix is addressing him in memory. The opening address recalls the unexpected and disembodied "O Tosco" of *Inferno* x.22, so seemingly unprepared are the words. For a moment the reader is unaware, as Dante and the reader in *Inferno* x were unaware, of the source of the address. [13]The opening lines of *Inferno* xx mark a clear break:

> Di nova pena mi conven far versi
> e dar matera al ventesimo canto
> de la prima canzon, ch'è d'i sommersi.   *Inf.*xx.1-3

[14]See *Par.*xvii.136-42 for "l'anime che son di fama note", as examples.

[15]The longest section of the canto, (31-87) is also divisible into a number of dynamic pieces pursuing an irregular narrative, but making for powerful dramatic expression.

[16]The following list to line 21 is a good example of Dante's technique in obtaining a special effect, in this case one of resonance in such groups as *on, mon, ond, omb*: S*imon m*ago, *bon*tate, de*on,con*vien, su*on*i, *mon*tati; *mond*o, f*ond*o, t*ond*o, *Non m*i, s*on, non, ogn'omo*; *o m*iseri, tr*omb*a, t*omb*a, pi*omb*a, s*omm*a; c*omp*arte; m*ol*t'anni.

[17]Dante's name in fact occurs at *Purgatorio* xxx.55.

[18]The last part of this account is taken at times word for word from Foster, p. 53. Scott gives an exhaustive account of lines 16-21, pp. 471-9. See Foster, p. 52 and Scott passim for discussions of the early commentators. Foster argues sensibly that "battezzatori" means fonts, Scartazzini is equally reasonable in opting for priests. Scott (in a note on p. 471) is certain that "they were in fact places in which the priests administered baptism". It seems to me that if "battezzatori" means fonts, this makes "loco" less clear and partly redundant; but if "battezzatori" means pastors then "loco" or some such word becomes necessary to the sense. The relative "li quali" may refer to "quei" which refers to "fori", but if however it refers to "battezzatori", and this is taken to mean priests, then the meaning "rupp'io" and "v'annegava" must be carefully examined. There is evidence to suggest that "annegava" may be the verb "abnegava" as the form is found in thirteenth-century prose, but for this to be worth pursuing, some meaning such as reprimand or censure would have to be found for Dante's use of "rompere". In interpreting "sganni" it is clear that Dante is casting himself in a role opposed to the deceiver. In this canto Boniface (56) fulfils that role and as Foster, pp. 54-5, notes, "a kind of anti-Church is being depicted", which it is Dante's task to discredit and indeed shatter by his censure. L. Spitzer, "Two Dante Notes", *Romanic Review,* 34 (1943), 248-62, and S. Noakes, "Dino Compagni and the Vow in San Giovanni: *Inferno* XIX, 16-21" in *Dante Studies,* 86 (1968), 41-63, make

determined efforts to solve the problem of line 21 and they certainly help broaden and define the readers' terms of reference. Scott gives a complete account of the meanings of "suggel" and "sganni" but in the final analysis the line has the simplicity and inscrutability of an oracular utterance.

[19] As in other encounters, for instance *Inferno* v and x, Virgil does not anticipate the dramatic effect by revealing the identity of the spirit Dante is about to meet.

[20] See notes 5 and 6 above.

[21] C. S. Lewis, "Dante's Similes" in *Studies in Medieval and Renaissance Literature* (Cambridge, 1966), pp. 64-77 (pp. 69-70).

[22] See the note to Scott, p. 466.

[23] For Clement V and Philip the Fair of France, see sonnet no. 82 in the edition of *Dante's Lyric Poetry* by K. Foster and P. Boyde, 2 vols (Oxford, 1967). Clement is also attacked in *Paradiso* xvii.82, xxvii.58, xxx.142-8.

[24] Of Clement Nicholas says that he will be a new Jason and favoured by the King of France. The Jason here was a biblical one and not the Argonaut described in *Inferno* xviii as full of "inganno"; this Jason was a high priest who bought his office as narrated in Maccabees, though the correspondence of "inganno" in *Inferno* xviii and xix provides a link between the cantos.

[25] See Foster, p. 63.

[26] This was one of only three passages in the *Divina Commedia* censored by the Spanish Inquisition, see Scott, p. 467.

[27] Lines 106-11 make use of Apocalypse 17:15.

[28] Constantine is to be met with in *Paradiso* xx. Constantine the Great was reputed to have given temporal possessions to Pope Sylvester I. See *Inferno* xxvii.94-5.

[29] *Mon.*III.X. 1-6 and *Paradiso* vi.

[30] Synonyms for legs or parts of the leg used in this canto, including repetitions, are in order: "piedi", "gambe", "grosso", "piante", "giunte", "calcagni", "punte", "zanca", "piedi" (23 and 64), "piè" (79 and 81), "piote".

[31]Foster, p. 56.

[32]Musa, supported in part by the note to J. Scott, pp. 463-4, who refers to E. N. Kaulbach's study in *Dante Studies,* 86 (1968), 127-35, makes the identification in *Essays on Dante,* p. 170. See also M. Musa and A. G. Hatcher, "Lucifer's Legs", *PMLA,* 79 (1964), 191-9, and C. S. Singleton's discussion in his article, "*Inferno* XIX: O Simon Mago!", *MLN,* 80 (1966), 92-9.

[33]*Inf.* xxxiv.90: "e vidili le gambe in sú tenere."

[34]In Acts 8, Peter said to Simon: "Pecunia tua tecum sit in perditionem, quoniam donum Dei existimasti pecunia possideri."

[35]Foster, p. 57.

[36]There are some particular features of Dante's use of language in this canto which are worth noting. Principally he seems to use a technique of intensification. This he achieves by repetition and progression. The use of synonyms for riches has already been noticed in the quotation from Foster, see note 9, and the repetition of words meaning foot and legs has also been referred to, see note 30. Other words to be repeated, sometimes as different parts of speech, are "mal", "bel", "fondo", "chiavi", "pastor", "pietra", "argine", "ripa", "scoglio". Different forms of the following are also used: "buon", "virtù", "Pietro", "re", "saper", "soave", "piace", "somma", "credi", "torre". Note also "rupp'io" and "rotto". Most of these repetitions are to be expected but others which have a particularly intensifying effect seem to reflect a conscious stylistic decision; "puttana" in *Inferno* xviii to "puttaneggiar" has already been noticed, but see also "Simon" and "simoneggiando"; "fiammeggia" and "fiamma"; "fori" and "foracchiato"; "guizzavan" and "guizzando"; "piangeva" and "pianto"; "re" and "regi"; "trista" and "attrista"; "roggia" and "rossi"; "orsa" and "orsatti".

Inferno XXVI: A Personal Appreciation

G. Singh

In his *The Idea of Great Poetry,* before setting out to deal with Dante's *Divina Commedia,* Lascelles Abercrombie makes this disclaimer: "There are", he says, "many recognized indications of insanity: none more reliable, I suppose, than the conviction of having something new to say about Dante. You will not, I hope, think that I am qualifying for the attentions of the alienists now". I could not agree with this more and for obvious reasons, for apart from the fact that I am not a Dante specialist, I have nothing new to say either about Dante or about the *Ulysses* canto which, like most great cantos in Dante, has long been one of those arguments apropos of which Dr. Johnson said that one can say nothing new that is true and nothing true that is new. Having said this, I hope I have sufficiently forestalled any charge of leading you to suppose that what I am going to say is something that most of you would not have come to see for yourselves.

If one were to single out one particular canto in the *Inferno,* or even in the whole of the *Divina Commedia,* where both

what separates our world from Dante's and what links it with
that world, are so closely interknit, one would be hard put to
choose a more appropriate one than the Ulysses canto. For not
only does Ulysses embody the link between the classical world
and Dante's, while foreshadowing the link between Dante's
world and the Renaissance, or between the Renaissance and
what followed, but also about the reasons for which Ulysses is
condemned and about Dante's and Virgil's respect for him, in
spite of his condemnation, there is something perennially
modern and perennially appealing. The fact is that in
condemning the protagonist, Dante seems no more convinced
than was Milton in condemning Lucifer and in robbing him in
the later books of *Paradise Lost* of the moral authority and
heroic significance he had conferred on him in the first two
books. Similarly, it seems to me that the suddenness with
which, in the last seven lines of the canto, the courage and
daring of Ulysses and of his few but loyal shipmates,

> . . . 'quella compagna
> picciola da la qual non fui diserto,'   101-2

meets with irretrievable disaster, with the sea wreaking havoc
on their boat and engulfing it and them, has something
arbitrary and inexplicable about it, whether one calls it with
Croce "una misteriosa e religiosa forza della natura",[1] or one
calls it in Sapegno's words, "la ferrea ragione teologica di
Dante".[2]

> 'Noi ci allegrammo, e tosto tornò in pianto,
>   ché de la nova terra un turbo nacque
>   e percosse del legno il primo canto.
> Tre volte il fé girar con tutte l'acque;
>   a la quarta levar la poppa in suso
>   e la prora ire in giú, com' altrui piacque,
> infin che 'l mar fu sovra noi richiuso'.   136-42

In fact there is even something of unseemly haste about the way Dante dispatches Ulysses and his companions to their doom. The abrupt transition from joy to sorrow: "noi ci allegrammo, e tosto tornò in pianto" (136), and their complete helplessness in the face of their doom enact not only God's will, "com' altrui piacque" (141), but to some extent also Dante's who, before moving on to the next canto, wants to wash his hands, as speedily as possible, of the predestined end of Ulysses. It is not so much the end as the manner in which it is brought about that seems to lack plausibility. Nor does Dante himself seem to be as passionately convinced by the causes of such an end as both he and Virgil are convinced about Ulysses's personal courage. Hence, what more convenient and summary device than that of a sudden storm through which the will of Providence is carried out. And yet what an uncharacteristic end for the hero of the Trojan war as well as of the "cento milia perigli" (112-13), as he himself legitimately boasts: no fight, no bravery, no heroism, as if Ulysses and his followers had possessed all these qualities in vain, simply death by water. And it is no consolation to know that Dante erects, as Manfredi Porena points out, "a sepulchre in the midst of the infinite ocean such as nobody has ever had before".[3] In a certain way the helplessness of Ulysses and his shipmates reflects Dante's own helplessness, his helplessness in view of what the philosophical and the theological plan and structure of his work demanded. One therefore feels more inclined to agree with Croce when he points out that Ulysses's end originates not from a poetic motive but from a didactic and practical one or with Professor Stanford when he calls Dante's "inexorable verdict . . . propagandist, not moralistic or judicial"[4] than with Fubini for whom Dante's classical taste "mirabilmente si accorda con la sua severa concezione religiosa, così come si accorda senza dissidio o contrasto nel suo cuore l'ammirazione per l'eroe e la sommissione alla volontà di Dio."[5]

Ulysses and Diomedes were, of course, guilty of having acted upon the dictum that all is fair in love and war, and they are punished for having resorted to fraud in order to conquer their enemies. But in a canto which starts with Dante's invective against the moral and political corruption of Florence, an invective which exemplifies the fusion of Dante's poetic eloquence and moral irony, it is Ulysses's account of what he undertook to achieve that constitutes the moral counterweight, as it were, to that corruption. In fact both the moral and the poetic core of this canto is very much tied up with *that* as well as with the contradiction implicit in Dante's celebrating what in the end he is forced to condemn. The invective against Florence fits in well with the Ulysses episode, in so far as in each case Dante's involvement is of a deeply personal as well as moral nature. What he considers to be "il varco folle d'Ulisse" (*Par*.xxvii.82-3) is no less a tribute to Ulysses's feat than a reproof of it. His own admiration for Ulysses comes out not only in his intense desire to communicate with him, but also in the way his style takes on a lyric colouring as well as a moral sublimity. That is why it is not true to say, as John Addington Symonds remarks in his *Introduction to the Study of Dante,* that it is Ulysses and Diomedes who "approach Dante, and like Greeks anxious for celebrity, show willingness to talk".[6] As to the bitterness and irony behind his invective against Florence, they are, of course, inspired by Dante's love and esteem for his native city. And it is this sense of honour, both apropos of Florence and of Ulysses, that gives meaning to the whole canto. Dante's concern for the honour of Florence as voiced in the opening lines of this canto not only makes Florence's shame his own, but somehow also sets the tone for what Ulysses is going to relate:

> Godi, Fiorenza, poi che se' sí grande
>   che per mare e per terra batti l'ali,
>   e per lo 'nferno tuo nome si spande!
> Tra li ladron trovai cinque cotali
>   tuoi cittadini onde mi ven vergogna,
>   e tu in grande orranza non ne sali.   1-6

Dante's shame is all the greater because the five Florentines he met in the preceding *bolgia* belonged to noble families, which leads him to prophesy great misfortunes as a punishment for Florence. However, his prophesying is not so much the result of an implicit moral or metaphysical belief that evil cannot go unpunished, as the outcome of his personal involvement in the vicissitudes of Florence, which makes that punishment a necessity for his own soul. The longer this punishment is delayed, the more he feels it will weigh upon him as he grows older. But the punishment he would mete out to Florence is something he already sees being administered to those, the five members of the Florentine nobility among them, who are in the eighth circle.

Thus Dante's personal involvement in the history and political fortunes of Florence invests him with a dual role in this canto: his role as a poet and his role as being himself a protagonist alongside of Ulysses and Diomedes. That is why he listens to Ulysses's account, not as a passive listener, but as one whose moral and political vicissitudes bear a certain similarity to those of the Greek hero. Dante's life of exile, entailing as it did countless privations and sacrifices, including separation from his wife and children, was the direct outcome of his political beliefs and loyalties. But behind such beliefs and loyalties there was the spirit, not so much of partisanship, as of a lofty vision and ideal of liberty and unity both for his native city and for his country as a whole. And an even greater and more significant factor in Dante's life and personality was his love of truth and knowledge for their own sake and in the widest and profoundest sense of the term. Of course, Dante could not always reconcile this love with his theological assumptions, but the contrast between the two only served to heighten his sense of the reality of each. In Dante, Foscolo rightly points out, "il piacere di conoscere e propugnare il vero, e di sentirsi atto a farlo suonare per fin dal sepolcro, è sì acuto da preponderare a tutte le amaritudini, onde per consueto la vita de' sommi ingegni è saturata, non tanto per la freddezza e

l'invidia dell'umana schiatta, quanto per le cocenti passioni de'
loro proprii cuori."[7] No doubt such "burning passions" were in
each individual case markedly different, as was the manner in
which both Dante and Ulysses sought to realize or rather
sublimate them. Nevertheless there is a comparable intensity of
commitment behind what they set out to achieve. Moreover it
is Dante's awareness of such kinship with Ulysses that makes
him implicitly realize the difference between his own lot and
that of Ulysses.

For whereas Ulysses had no guide to follow other than
himself and no counsel to go by other than that of his own
instinct, indeed one can say of him, to use Swinburne's words,
that "save his own soul he hath no star", Dante enjoys the
unfailing support and guidance of Virgil, so that the more
difficult his situation, the more readily he turns to him for the
help which is invariably given:

>   . . . su per le scalee
> che n'avea fatte iborni a scender pria,
> rimontò 'l duca mio e trasse me.   13-15

In Ulysses's case, on the other hand, no help is sought and none
obtained. His pride and self-confidence are such as to prevent
him from seeking any help from any quarter, even if such help
were forthcoming. The quality of his self-dependence and self-
assurance may be regarded as Titanic, especially if one
compares it with Dante's own prudence and self-restraint and
his instinctive belief that whatever he might achieve is in a large
measure the outcome of divine grace and of influences beyond
his control.

> Allor mi dolsi, e ora mi ridoglio
>   quando drizzo la mente a ciò ch'io vidi,
>   e piú lo 'ngegno affreno ch'i' non soglio,
> perché non corra che virtú nol guidi;
>   sí che, se stella bona o miglior cosa
>   m'ha dato 'l ben, ch'io stessi nol m'invidi.   19-24

The moral sagaciousness behind such self-restraint stands
Dante in good stead not only during his journey through Hell,
but also in his lifetime without, however, its exercising any
debilitating influence on his will and passion. How healthy
such a curb is, both spiritually and pragmatically, is illustrated
by the contrast that in some respects Dante's destiny presents
with that of Ulysses, a contrast for which Dante prepares us in
the lines quoted above. For in Ulysses's case it is precisely the
absence of any curb or restraint as well as his invincible desire
to know and explore, or, to quote Tennyson's "Ulysses", lines
31-2:

> To follow knowledge like a sinking star,
> Beyond the utmost bound of human thought.

It is this desire that constitutes both his strength and his
weakness, his claim to glory and his ruin.

Having cautiously acquainted himself with the extent to
which he should follow the bent of his genius, Dante turns to
the flames he and Virgil see in this chasm — flames as
numerous as the fireflies a peasant sees in a valley from the top
of a hill:

> Quante 'l villan ch'al poggio si riposa,
>   nel tempo che colui che 'l mondo schiara
>   la faccia sua a noi tien meno ascosa,
> come la mosca cede a la zanzara,
>   vede lucciole giú per la vallea,
>   forse colà dov' e' vendemmia e ara. 25-30

While the sense of numerical multitudinousness itself
contributes to the commonplaceness or non-particularity of
the sin in question, the relaxed setting of a rural scene offsets
the solemnity of the episode that is going to be recounted, in
such a way as to make us feel better disposed to grasp the
import, not so much of the sin committed, as of the sinner
committing it.

Dante catches sight of a particular flame with a double tip, and asks Virgil who is hidden in it. When Virgil observes that it conceals the spirits of Ulysses and Diomedes who "cosí insieme a la vendetta vanno come a l'ira" (56-7), Dante feels an irresistible desire to communicate with them, as can be seen from the way he implores Virgil to let him do so:

> . . . 'maestro, assai ten priego
> e ripriego, che 'l priego vaglia mille,
> che non mi facci de l'attender niego
> fin che la fiamma cornuta qua vegna;
> vedi che del disio ver' lei mi piego!'   65-9

Unlike most of the major characters in *Inferno*, whom either Dante knew personally or about whom he knew through some other source, Ulysses was somebody to whose classical name and fame he was drawn solely in order to celebrate those ideals and aspirations of his own personality which Ulysses's personality seemed to represent. In Ulysses, Umberto Bosco rightly points out, Dante defends himself, for he too did not let himself be affected by family ties, and instead obeyed the voice of duty.[8] In a way his desire to hear Ulysses speak is itself a measure of his moral esteem for him as well as a token of his faith in such virtues as courage, daring and curiosity. For Ulysses embodies these virtues so impressively that even his sin, however grave, cannot efface them. In regarding Dante's prayer as being "degna di molta loda" (70-1), Virgil indirectly reveals his own desire to talk to Ulysses, and at the same time he inculcates in Dante a certain awe towards Ulysses, by asking him to refrain from doing so. His counsel to Dante: "fa che la tua lingua si sostegna" (72), is meant not so much to dampen Dante's enthusiasm as to translate it into a more fruitful course of action in order to elicit Ulysses's response:

> 'Lascia parlare a me, ch'i' ho concetto
> ciò che tu vuoi; ch'ei sarebbero schivi,
> perch' e' fuor greci, forse del tuo detto'.   73-5

Virgil's suspicion that Ulysses and Diomedes might be reluctant to talk to Dante because they are Greeks alludes to the belief commonly held in the Middle Ages that the Greeks were a proud and haughty race. In the case of Ulysses and Diomedes the justification for their pride is all the more cogent in so far as they brought about, or helped to bring about, the destruction of the proud and beautiful city of Troy, "superbum Ilium" (*Aeneid* 3,2-3), reducing it as Pound says in his *Cantos* to a "heap of smouldering boundary stones". Virgil's offer to talk to Ulysses rather than letting Dante do so brings out his own sense of importance as a Latin poet, a poet who was much more familiar with the ancient Greek world than was Dante. Both these reasons serve to heighten our sense of awe and anticipation at the colloquy between Virgil and Ulysses.

When Virgil apostrophizes Ulysses and Diomedes, he addresses them not as the sinners they are, but as illustrious personages, and his mode of doing so, that is to say, his style and technique as well as the substance of what he says, shows him to be a master of poetic elocution as well as of persuasion. Reminding them of what he wrote about them in his epic poem, he not only flatters them, but also establishes his own claim as a poet. Homage to them is to some extent an implicit homage to his own art:

'O voi che siete due dentro ad un foco,
   s'io meritai di voi mentre ch'io vissi,
   s'io meritai di voi assai o poco
quando nel mondo li alti versi scrissi,
   non vi movete; ma l'un di voi dica
   dove, per lui, perduto a morir gissi'.   79-84

Virgil's assumption that Ulysses and Diomedes would be flattered by the fact of their having been mentioned in the *Aeneid* is a proof that he regards them, and justly, as men who not only value fame, courage and the desire for knowledge above everything else, but who are also conscious of their own superiority.

His solemn entreaty has the desired effect. Ulysses, "lo maggior corno" (85), greater than Diomedes both in terms of personal importance and in terms of responsibility for the sin and the degree of sinfulness attached to his deeds, starts speaking. His succinct account of what happened, constituting "the condensed and intensely exciting narrative",[9] as T.S. Eliot calls it, begins with an almost brusque directness and matter-of-factness of tone which is in keeping with his sense of self-importance as well as with the tragic sombreness of what he is going to relate. In other words, although a sinner, his sense of his own dignity permeates all he says and his manner of saying it. And what he says is singularly free from any trace of regret or remorse, wrong or grievance. He accedes to Virgil's request without any fuss and goes straight to the heart of the matter, thereby exemplifying that superiority of his character and personality to which Virgil's own flattering approach to him testifies. Both in the choice of detail, fact and circumstance by means of which the story is related and in the nature of the style and diction used, there is an aristocratic firmness and decisiveness of tone which brings out the triple force of Dante's style: its vividness, succinctness and concreteness. The descriptive and geographical detail, for instance, does something more than merely contribute to the specificity and realism of the narration, conferring on the places and cities mentioned such an evocative appeal that the real and the pictorial acquire a strange and elusive character. Thus, for instance, Circe's abode "là presso a Gaeta" (92), the African and European coasts of the Mediterranean:

> 'L'un lito e l'altro vidi infin la Spagna,
>   fin nel Morrocco, e l'isola d'i Sardi,
>   e l'altre che quel mare intorno bagna,'   103-5

or the dramatically simple allusions to Seville and Ceuta,

>   'da la man destra mi lasciai Sibilia,
>   da l'altra già m'avea lasciata Setta,'   110-11

constitute not merely the geographical landmarks in Ulysses's journey, but also the spiritual ones, both measuring the distance he has already covered and enticing him towards his imagined goal.

The sea itself, "l'alto mare aperto" (100), which plays a crucial role in Ulysses's journey and which puts an end to his career, is a symbol of his immeasurable pride and ambition as well as of his loftiness of purpose and single-mindedness. In a way it acts the part both of an antagonist and a tempter, spurring him on in his fatal course both by virtue of the wanderlust it inspires in him as a traveller and an explorer, and by virtue of the challenge its limitlessness offers to his own almost limitless powers. The epitomic neatness with which Ulysses characterizes the various stages of his journey is not only an indication of the speed with which he is covering his ground, but also a measure of his zeal and enthusiasm, of that "ardore"

> 'ch'i' ebbi a divenir del mondo esperto
> e de li vizi umani e del valore.'   98-9

But an even more significant measure of Ulysses's ardour than the one constituted by the physical landmarks is the one constituted by his love for his only son, his affection and duty towards his old father and his wife. But even these ties and considerations fail to restrain him from the journey his heart and mind are set on and to which his past life as well as the indomitable forces of his own nature and personality have irrevocably committed him:

> 'né dolcezza di figlio, né la pieta
>   del vecchio padre, né 'l debito amore
>   lo qual dovea Penelopè far lieta,
> vincer potero dentro a me l'ardore
>   ch'i' ebbi a divenir del mondo esperto
>   e de li vizi umani e del valore.'   94-9

Still another measure of this ardour is the inadequacy of means and equipment at his disposal:

> 'sol con un legno e con quella compagna
> picciola da la qual non fui diserto.'   101-2

The more meagre the means, the more heroic appears the task he and his companions have undertaken. There is something magnificently desperate about such an undertaking and the fact that he can count on the loyalty of his men to the very last does not make that undertaking less arduous or less desperate. Ulysses himself is indeed fully aware of this; in fact both as the leader and as the originator of the plan he could not have been otherwise. He is also acutely conscious of the moral and physical limitations in himself and in his companions, as he observes in one of the most poignantly pregnant lines in the whole canto:

> 'Io e' compagni eravam vecchi e tardi.'   106

In the phrase "vecchi e tardi" — which is an Ovidian echo — the words "vecchi" and "tardi" act upon each other as cause and effect. Moreover, the word "tardi" also suggests not merely the opposite of *veloce* or *in fretta*, but also of *presto* or *in tempo*. Thus the undertones of regret and wistfulness in this line are due not merely to the realization on the part of Ulysses and his companions that they are slow in their movements, because old, but also that it is too late for them to undertake such a task. However, neither the feeling of regret nor that of wistfulness betrays any slackening of the will to undertake the journey beyond the Pillars of Hercules, beyond, that is,

> 'dov' Ercule segnò li suoi riguardi
> acciò che l'uom piú oltre non si metta.'   108-9

There is a heroic disregard on Ulysses's part of the unforeseeable hazards that such a course might involve. But so far as his shipmates are concerned, a natural consequence of their being "vecchi e tardi" is a greater degree of instinctive prudence on their part, and tied up with it a certain feeling of hesitation. Not that they give vent to this feeling, but as a leader Ulysses is sagacious enough to intuit it. That is why in his exhortative discourse, or what he calls "questa orazion picciola" (122), he seeks to hearten them and reassure them, and in so doing displays an even greater degree of mastery in the art of persuasion than did Virgil when he succeeded in persuading Ulysses to talk to him.

Ulysses himself helps us gauge the effect of his speech on his companions:

> 'Li miei compagni fec' io sí aguti,
>   con questa orazion picciola, al cammino,
>   che a pena poscia li avrei ritenuti.'   121-3

In fact it takes him no more than nine lines to achieve this effect, but they are lines which have the charged pithiness and simplicity of Dante's poetry at its best and most intense — poetry in which the moral authority and earnestness of what is said admirably inform the inspiring austerity of style and diction:

> 'O frati', dissi, 'che per cento milia
>   perigli siete giunti a l'occidente,
>   a questa tanto picciola vigilia
> d'i nostri sensi ch'è del rimanente,
>   non vogliate negar l'esperïenza,
>   di retro al sol, del mondo sanza gente.
> Considerate la vostra semenza:
>   fatti non foste a viver come bruti,
>   ma per seguir virtute e canoscenza'.   112-20

As one who will be condemned for the sin of fraud and unscrupulous astuteness, that is the misuse of one's intelligence in order to secure an unfair advantage over one's friend or enemy, Ulysses resorts to a somewhat cunning device in overcoming whatever diffidence he encounters in his companions, and in exacting their wholehearted loyalty to him and to the venture they are going to embark upon. In the first place his accosting them as "frati" makes those he actually leads feel as if they are on a par with him. Secondly, his reminding them of the numerous hazards and hardships which they have already undergone with such fortitude and perseverance makes them not only proud of themselves and of what they have done, but also desirous to achieve even more, or as Francesco Torraca points out, "di non mostrarsi minori di se stessi".[10] Thirdly, and most importantly, Ulysses uses the art of poetic persuasion to a philosophical end and the dialectics of moral and philosophical reasoning to a poetic end.

Take, for instance, the image, which is both morally pregnant and concretely realized, through which he epitomizes what life in all its brevity and precariousness means and what it comes to mean particularly when a considerable portion of it has already been lived out: "questa tanto picciola vigilia d'i nostri sensi" (114-5). It is by not saying anything about how the "vigilia d'i nostri sensi" is so much more than what it says that Dante can turn such a partial and reductive account of life into something at once familiar and strange, poignant and promising. Such an image cannot but fire the hearts and imagination of Ulysses's companions and make them all the more covetous of the prize offered: "l'esperïenza, di retro al sol, del mondo sanza gente" (116-7). But while there is something positively concrete about the phrase "negar l'esperïenza" (116), referring, as it does, to the "senses" both in their literal and in their symbolic meaning, the object of that experience is something at once vague and indefinable and therefore all the more tantalizing: "the unpeopled world behind the Sun". For such insatiably avid explorers and adventurers like Ulysses and his companions what lure could have been greater? To their thirst for knowledge is added what Yeats calls the fascination of what's difficult. Thus, in order to help his companions overcome an instinctive fear of the unknown and of those regions where nobody has ever set foot, Ulysses has recourse to a moral as well as psychological expedient. He makes them realize the true significance of all their human destiny and reminds them of their superiority over brutes. There is no more impressive way of assserting this superiority than to follow virtue and knowledge. Ulysses does not so much equate "virtute" and "canoscenza" as regard them as interdependent and complementary:

'Considerate la vostra semenza:
    fatti non foste a viver come bruti,
    ma per seguir virtute e canoscenza'.   118-20

The moral weight and authority behind the imperative-cum-imploratory force of the verb "considerate" is not contradicted, nor even weakened by the fact that in Dante's theological scheme Ulysses is a sinner and has not himself always followed "virtute". But he seems to be making up for what he has lost by not following "virtute", by following "canoscenza". It is this as well as his readiness to put into practice what he preaches to others, that stands out in this canto, not only enhancing his credibility as a leader, but also adding to the plausibility of what he says. It is not, as Bosco acutely observes, "the fascination of the unknown or of the mysterious which tempts him; but on the contrary the need to annul the mysterious in himself by conquering it".[11]

By this stage his companions are so eager to go ahead that even if he had wanted to, it would have been hard for him to restrain them. The very fact that Ulysses even gives any consideration to such a hypothesis goes to prove that although he was fully aware of his responsibility in the matter, he neither was nor could have been in a position to forestall the impact of

his speech. No wonder he himself seems surprised at his companions' reaction to it while nonetheless assuming implicitly
full responsibility for what, inspired or rather instigated by
him, they are capable of doing.

In the remaining nineteen lines Ulysses describes the last
stage of their sea journey before meeting the fated but unforeseeable end. The zeal and decisiveness with which they
turn their backs on the world and on humanity and head
towards the east is reflected in the fast movement of the oars:

> 'e volta nostra poppa nel mattino,
>   de' remi facemmo ali al folle volo,
>   sempre acquistando dal lato mancino.'   124-6

Their speed devours time as well as space; becomes so to speak,
a measure of their perseverance and determination. What they
see   through   their   constantly   changing   bearings   and
perspectives merges with what they imagine or visualize.
Glimpses   of   different   worlds   and   hemispheres   impress
themselves upon them, as they chart their way through seas
hitherto unsailed, with only the moon and the stars looking
down upon them with their old familiar looks:

> 'Tutte le stelle già de l'altro polo
>   vedea la notte, e 'l nostro tanto basso,
>   che non surgëa fuor del marin suolo.
> Cinque volte racceso e tante casso
>   lo lume era di sotto da la luna,
>   poi che 'ntrati eravam ne l'alto passo.'   127-32

At long last they come within sight of the Mount of Purgatory
which augurs well for them and they are happy for a while. But
soon their happiness turns into gloom and tragedy. Ulysses
relates what happened with the minimum of factual detail and
the only reason that is given for the tragedy is summed up in the
phrase: "com' altrui piacque" (141). Although Dante puts this

phrase into his mouth, it conveys a sense of resignation that ill accords with the ethos that Ulysses's character and personality embody. A sense of inexorable doom and finality weighs upon the closing lines which relate how Ulysses's quest comes to a tragic end. And implicitly underlying that end is a sense of moral perplexity which, among other things, makes for the poetic intensity of this canto.

If in his poem "Ulysses" (lines 7-11) Tennyson celebrates the courage, determination and adventurous spirit of his hero:

> . . . all times I have enjoyed
> Greatly, have suffered greatly, both with those
> That loved me, and alone; on shore, and when
> Through scudding drifts the rainy Hyades
> Vext the dim sea: I am become a name;

it was left to a modern poet like Ezra Pound in *The Cantos* to voice the sense of waste and loss suffered by Ulysses's companions, a sense of waste that enables us to assess both the tragic and the heroic, the sublime and the pathetic aspects of all that was involved in Ulysses's "ardore . . . a divenire del mondo esperto de li vizi umani e del valore" (97-9):

> 'They that died in the whirlpool
> 'And after many vain labours,
> 'Living by stolen meat, chained to the rowingbench,
> 'That he should have a great fame
>   'And lie by night with the goddess?
> 'Their names are not written in bronze
>   'Nor their rowing sticks set with Elpenor's;
> 'Nor have they mound by sea-bord.
>   'That saw never the olives under Spartha
> 'With the leaves green and then not green,
>   'The click of light in their branches;
> 'That saw not the bronze hall nor the ingle
> 'Nor lay there with the queen's waiting maids,

'Nor had they Circe to couch-mate, Circe Titania,
'Nor had they meats of Kalüpso
'Or her silk skirts brushing their thighs
'Give! What were they given?
                                        Ear-wax.
'Poison and ear-wax,
                        and a salt grave by the bull-field,
'*neson amumona*, their heads like sea crows in the foam,
'Black splotches, sea-weed under lightning;
'Canned beef of Apollo, ten cans for a boat load.'
Ligur' aoide.

                                                          Canto XX

In tone, ethos and substance this passage could not have been
further from Dante's canto. And yet, as in the case of his
"Homage to Sextus Propertius", it is the very differences, at
times so sharp and radical as almost to border on parody, that
bring out Pound's indebtedness to Dante, and the critical no
less than the creative way that indebtedness is translated into
an art that both looks back to Dante and at the same time looks
away from him. For Pound's avowed aim was "to write an epic
poem which begins 'In the Dark Forest', crosses the Purgatory
of human error, and ends in the light, and 'fra i maestri di color
che sanno' ",[12] a patently Dantesque aim, except for the
difference that whereas Dante's descent is into hell, Pound's is
into the historical past. As regards the character of Ulysses,
even though Pound thought him guilty of the theft of the
Palladium, he could not help admiring him, any more than
could Dante, for his extraordinary courage, ambition and
resourcefulness. Ulysses may have been guilty of the theft of
the Palladium, but he was not guilty of what Pound considered
to be an even greater sin, namely that of not doing instead of
doing:

            But to have done instead of not doing
                    this is not vanity
            To have, with decency, knocked

That a Blunt should open
   To have gathered from the air a live tradition
or from a fine old eye the unconquered flame
This is not vanity.
   Here error is all in the not done,
all in the diffidence that faltered.

Canto LXXXI

That in my conclusion I should have briefly referred to Dante's impact on Pound is itself a proof, if proof were needed, of the perennial modernity of Dante's poetry and its special relevance to twentieth-century poetry.

Notes

[1]B. Croce, *La poesia di Dante* (Bari, 1921), p. 98 (p. 95 in the 1966 edition).

[2]N. Sapegno ed., *Inferno* (Florence, 1975), p. 285.

[3]M. Porena, "Il canto di Ulisse", *Rivista d'Italia* (Rome, 1907); reprinted in M. Porena, *La mia Lectura Dantis* (Naples, 1932), pp. 87-112.

[4]W. B. Stanford, *The Ulysses Theme* (Oxford, 1954), p. 179.

[5]M. Fubini, *Due studi danteschi* (Florence, 1951).

[6]J. A. Symonds, *An Introduction to the Study of Dante* (London, 1897), p. 167.

[7]U. Foscolo, "Parallelo fra Dante e il Petrarca", [paragraph] XVI, *Saggi letterari,* ed. M. Fubini (Turin, 1925). A different reading is to be found in U. Foscolo, *Saggi critici*, ed. E. Bottasso, second edition (Turin, 1962), p. 232. In U. Foscolo, *Essays on Petrarch* (London, 1823), p. 201, the passage reads:

"The gratification of knowing and asserting the truth, and of being able to make it resound even from their graves, is so keen as to outbalance all the vexations to which the life of men of genius is generally doomed, not so much by the coldness and envy of mankind, as by the burning passions of their own hearts."

[8]"In Ulisse Dante difende se stesso che, come sappiamo, non fu trattenuto dai suoi affetti familiari quando si trattò di seguire, a costo dell'esilio, la voce del suo dovere verso se stesso", U. Bosco, *Inferno* (Turin, 1967), p. 194.

[9]In his essay on Tennyson's *In Memoriam* in T. S. Eliot, *Selected Essays* (London, 1951), p. 331.

[10]Quoted by N. Sapegno, see note 2, p. 294 (p. 301 in the 1955 edition).

[11]"Non è il fascino dell'ignoto, del mistero, che lo tenta; ma al contrario il bisogno di annullare in sé il mistero, di conquistarlo", U. Bosco, see note 8, p. 195.

[12]*Inf*.iv.131 describes Aristotle as "'l maestro di color che sanno" and this is adapted here by E. Pound, "Introduction to the Economic Nature of the United States" in *Selected Prose,* ed. William Cookson (London, 1973), p. 137.

The Context of Inferno XXXIII: Bocca, Ugolino, Fra Alberigo

C. Salvadori Lonergan

The political theme undoubtedly enters the *Commedia* in its second line, being one of the forces of darkness in Dante's "selva oscura". Ciacco brings it into the open in *Inferno* vi and it develops in a series of encounters throughout the *Inferno* until it finally reaches a powerful climax in Dante's exchanges with Bocca degli Abati, Ugolino della Gherardesca and Frate Alberigo.[1] While these episodes must be read in the wider context of the *Commedia*, that is in the context of Dante's militant action against avarice or *cupiditas*, and of his reforming zeal and plea for renewal, it is also effective to approach them in a more restricted framework, which epitomizes the overall plan. This framework may be visualized as a triangle in which the apex of Ugolino and his companion Ruggieri, is joined to the base formed by the supporting episodes of Bocca and Alberigo. Such a device as this is notional but it may be used towards a more precise understanding of the text.

Cocytus, where Virgil and Dante now are, is divided into Antenora, Caïna, Tolomea, Giudecca: traitors to country, kindred, hospitality, and allegiance; Bocca and Ugolino are in Antenora, Frate Alberigo and Branca Doria in Tolomea. The frozen zone of Cocytus contrasts markedly with the preceding area of Malebolge. Whereas before there had been activity, now there is stillness; before darkness predominated, now there is the sharp glow of ice; before several punishments were disgusting and nauseating, now, with the sinners immersed in ice, there is a sense of alienation caused by the hygiene that deep freezing induces. Here are condemned the traitors, those who broke a trust, who betrayed kinsmen, fatherland, party or political ideals, guests and benefactors. Generally speaking, they rejected *pietas*, understood as loyalty to the sources of human existence: father, fatherland, God as gratuitous benefactor. The traitors are frozen in an atmosphere of iciness. Postures differ, the extent of their immersion in the ice differs, but all are numb, congealed, a fitting punishment for those whose hearts had frozen. They are static from the paralysis of goodness within; the tears are frozen, the milk of human kindness had never flowed in their veins. Ice is the opposite of fire, it is an anti-life element. The words of Raffaello Ramat are appropriate here:

> I traditori hanno commesso l'*iniuria* piú grave, quella contro la legge che vuole il mondo umano retto secondo armonia di carità, e hanno perpetrato il delitto maggiore, quello contro la divinità dell'uomo: perciò sono nel punto piú lontano da Dio, presso a Lucifero, nel centro dell'universo; e come la malizia gelò nel loro spirito ogni senso razionale e naturale del vivere sociale, e i loro atti ne raggelarono il giusto processo, cosí sono immersi nella ghiaccia, simbolo estremo della anti-vita.[2]

Although Dante in the first line of *Inferno* xxxii deplores that his verses are inadequate to do justice to the terror of his vision, "S'io avessi le rime aspre e chiocce", the language is often harsh and grating and the images are fierce, even brutal. Even words not necessarily pejorative like "cuticagna" and "gorgiera" (*Inf*.xxxii.97 and 120) become so in the context. The images that predominate in *Inferno* xxxii and xxxiii are drawn mainly from the brute animal world. They are negative ones emphasizing its irrationality, its brutality, its uncontrollable physical violence. Tragically, these qualities are not confined to the world of animals, creatures without reason, but they are transferred to the world of men. The damned have "visi cagnazzi", dog-like faces (*Inf*.xxxii.70) and repeatedly their speaking is "latrare", to bark angrily; a movement of the foot becomes "pestare", to trample. Images of hunger abound but these are of gnawing, corroding, digging into, lacerating with one's teeth. Having once read it, one never forgets the "i' rodo" (*Inf*.xxxiii.8) of Ugolino. This repulsive physical violence is in a setting of stillness and ice that mirrors the condition of the heart. The range of emotions is both the "objective correlative"[3] of all this and its complete opposite. There is indifference, perplexity, anger, revulsion, intense hatred and also love that is equally intense. Dante takes the reader from the depth of the inhuman to the apex of the humane.

At the base of the triangle beginning at *Inferno* xxxii.76, Dante and Virgil are travelling on the lake in which the damned are frozen. Note the difference of levels and the apparent triviality of "passeggiando", strolling, a word that is most effective in removing all dignity from those at the feet of the travellers. The nearness of foot and head brings to mind a relevant verse from Genesis (3,15) referring to the crushing of Satan: "She shall crush thy head, and thou shalt lie in wait for her heel". It is relevant because it places before us the idea of Dante as God's agent, Dante in his role of minister of God on "a mission to a world astray";[4] a role that is all-important for an understanding of the final cantos of the *Inferno*. Dante strikes a sinner firmly with his foot: "forte percossi 'l piè nel viso ad una" (78), a deliberate, slow line loaded with emphases.

Each word is isolated. It is a gesture of violence that gives
momentum to a whole outburst of violence that will
characterize these episodes.

In the harsh exchange that ensues, the damned one refuses to
give his name, and Dante grabs him "per la cuticagna"(97), by
the scruff of the neck, twists his hair round in his hand and pulls
out several tufts, in an effort to force the sinner to reveal his
name. It is a traitor nearby who, appropriately, betrays Bocca's
identity with, among others, the interesting question: "qual
diavol ti tocca?" (108), what devil is at you?, and this devil is
Dante, whose role here is demonic. The devils in Hell are often
ministers of the justice of God. They punish and plunge more
deeply into the black boiling pitch those sinners who dare raise
their heads from it, they slash schismatics with a sword. Dante
here intensifies the punishment inflicted by God on Bocca degli
Abati, he is acting as minister, as upholder of the divine justice
that is violated by men, by traitors like Bocca.

Bocca degli Abati betrayed the Guelphs at the battle of
Montaperti, so that they lost the city of Florence. He is here
primarily to symbolize the perpetuation of the violence of man
to man, of the disruption and laceration of the God-willed
concourse of men. But the fact remains that Bocca represented
for Dante a political antagonist and this episode is an effort to
purify a political vendetta by raising it from the personal to the
level of the universal. In the context of Dante's role as minister,
this is acceptable, but the episode is disturbing because the
immediate reaction is to see it as an act of violence on a
personal enemy, who has been already made a victim in Hell, at
the hands of someone who has the advantage over him. A sense
of fair play is offended. But with Dante minister, there is also
Dante sinner and pilgrim, the Florentine political activist lost
in a dark wood of evil. In seeing Bocca degli Abati, there is an
act of self-recognition on the part of Dante; he sees what might
have been his fate had the "tre donne benedette" (*Inf.*ii.124) not
moved and sent Virgil to his aid. Hence the violence of the
gesture, it is a form of exorcizing that evil from himself. For

Dante as pilgrim the entire journey is a journey to self-knowledge, to the recognition of evil for what it is, without which knowledge, repentance is impossible. Dante dwells longest on those sins that are closest to his heart, and these seem to be the sins connected with politics and the political life. The *Inferno* never strays far from politics. There is a lengthy episode in Malebolge dealing with barratry, or swindling in official appointments, a crime which Dante was publicly accused of after he was exiled. Two cantos are given to false counselling, an activity for which Dante would have had ample opportunity, and the famous men whom Dante meets there were deeply involved in political intrigue: Ulysses and Guido da Montefeltro. *Inferno* xxxii and xxxiii are given over to traitors to country and to party, and though sinners like Frate Alberigo and Branca Doria are specifically condemned for treachery to guests, they were political figures, one a Guelph the other a Ghibelline, and their crimes were not totally dissociated from political implications. Other great figures of the *Inferno*, like Farinata and Pier della Vigna, are condemned for sins unrelated to politics, but the core of their discussions with Dante is their political life and public office.

Bocca's hysterical effort at vengeance on his fellows in Antenora (112-23) is ignored by Dante and his outburst is followed by what is merely a line of transition to the encounter with Count Ugolino and Archbishop Ruggieri: "Noi eravam partiti già da ello" (*Inf.*xxxii.124). It is not necessary here to elaborate on the labyrinthine intricacies of the political intrigues of the Pisan Ugolino della Gherardesca and his relative Ruggieri, who here is both Ugolino's victim and at the same time suffers with him the traitors' fate. Of them, Ugolino says: "dir non è mestieri" (*Inf.*xxxiii.18). It is sufficient to know that Ugolino betrayed in turn both Ghibellines and Guelphs and, when he placed his trust in Ruggieri, Ruggieri betrayed Ugolino to death. The image before the traveller at the end of *Inferno* xxxii is, in Dante's own words, "bestial" (133) and full of hatred. There are two creatures frozen in a hole, one,

Ugolino, raised slightly above the other, Ruggieri, so that he can gnaw at the skull of his victim: "'ve 'l cervel s'aggiugne con la nuca" (129). Twice there is an unusual use of an emphatic reflexive that emphasises a bond between punisher and victim: "Tidëo si rose" (130), "tu ti mangi" (134). The story that Ugolino is to tell is one of intense emotion, but Dante stresses an unemotional setting and alienates the story from its context. First there is the bare indifferent statement of the movement away from Bocca degli Abati already noted (*Inf*.xxxii.124) matched later by the unemotional "noi passammo oltre" (*Inf*.xxxiii.91) that forms the transition from Ugolino to Frate Alberigo. These two lines bring to mind Virgil's admonition to Dante "non ragioniam di lor, ma guarda e passa" (*Inf*.iii.51) about the uncommitted, the neutrals deeply scorned by Dante and relegated by him to the *Antinferno*. The attitude here is the same. The image of Ugolino and Ruggieri is repugnant to the sophisticated sense, but Dante gives the details without involvement and he uses a word that acts as a brake on reaction: the damned ones are "ghiacciati" (*Inf*.xxxii.125). They are frozen, all the creatures of Cocytus are, but the reminder at this point is very effective in lessening the sense of horror. It is a frozen chamber of horrors where human involvement seems impossible.

Detachment is reinforced by the classical simile taken from Statius:

> non altrimenti Tidëo si rose
>   le tempie a Menalippo per disdegno,
>   che quei faceva il teschio e l'altre cose. *Inf*.xxxii.130-2

Tydeus, referred to here, was one of the seven kings who besieged Thebes. He was mortally wounded by the Theban Menalippus, whom he then killed. While dying he gnawed the head of his killer in rage. The insertion of the classical story so far removed from Dante, Florence and Antenora, although visually apt in the narrative and apt dramatically, is yet another stage in detachment. It is at the beginning of the Ugolino encounter; another echo of Statius will end the episode. After his story to Dante, Ugolino resumes his gnawing of Ruggieri's head and does so "con li occhi torti" (*Inf.*xxxiii.76). These are the "lumina torva" of Statius's text.[5]

Dante strikes a bargain with Ugolino:

> 'dimmi 'l perché', diss'io, 'per tal convegno,
>   che se tu a ragion di lui ti piangi,
>   sappiendo chi voi siete e la sua pecca,
>   nel mondo suso ancora io te ne cangi,
>   se quella con ch'io parlo non si secca'.   *Inf.*xxxii.135-9

If Ugolino will tell the cause of his activity of hatred, Dante will avenge his name on earth. Canto xxxii is interrupted here by Dante although the narrative carries over. His reason is that he wishes to create a deliberate break between the setting of Ugolino's story and the story itself, which forms the bulk of *Inferno* xxxiii.

At this point, leaving aside the Ugolino episode, let us join the poets further on as they move from Antenora to Tolomea, to those who betrayed their guests. Taking up the narrative at xxxiii, 91, "noi passammo oltre", the first point to note is a statement that deals with a feature of the punishment of Tolomea:

> Lo pianto stesso lí pianger non lascia,
>   e 'l duol che truova in su li occhi rintoppo,
>   si volge in entro a far crescer l'ambascia.   94-6

The sinners are deprived of the relief of tears, the tears they shed freeze in the sockets of their eyes so that sorrow is intensified as it flows inwards. Dante then adds:

> E avvegna che, sí come d'un callo,
>   per la freddura ciascun sentimento
>   cessato avesse del mio viso stallo.   100-2

He refers to the callousness or absence of feeling in his own face caused by the intense cold; but this freezing of all emotion could be referred, appropriately, to his inner state. The only air he feels is that caused by the beating wings of Lucifer, for he and Virgil are now close to the source of evil.

> E un de' tristi de la fredda crosta
> gridò a noi: 'O anime crudeli . . . '   109-10

One of the damned, assuming that these moving downwards are worse sinners than he, addresses them as "anime crudeli" and begs them to relieve his suffering somewhat by removing the ice from his eye sockets. Dante's controversial reply offering to go to the bottom of the ice if the sinner reveals his identity and Dante does not relieve him, is:

> . . . 'Se vuo' ch'i' ti sovvegna,
> dimmi chi se', e s'io non ti disbrigo,
> al fondo de la ghiaccia ir mi convegna.'   115-17

It would be jesuitical or sophistical to say that Dante here is honest because he knows he has to go to the bottom of the pit and therefore he is, indirectly, telling the sinner that he will not help him. To be blunt and honest, Dante's intention is to force the damned soul to reveal his identity and in order to reach this end he is prepared to deceive him. Because Frate Alberigo is successfully deceived he gives more information than was requested.

Alberigo was a *frate gaudente,* one of the "jovial friars" so called because of the easy life in which they indulged. Properly, they were the knights of *Maria Vergine gloriosa,* an order founded in 1261 for the protection of the weak and for mediation in political feuds. Alberigo is here damned for killing relatives at a banquet that he gave in their honour: "i' son quel de le frutta del mal orto" (*Inf.*xxxiii.119). At an agreed signal, when in fact he called for the fruit to be served, the hired assassins entered the banqueting hall and slaughtered the guests. Alberigo's comment on his suffering is ironic, an indication of his jovial personality as a *frate gaudente:* "qui riprendo dattero per figo" (120), here in hell I have got date for fig, a saying still in use to indicate getting more than one bargained for, as the date is considered the more exotic fruit.

Dante's reaction to the information is one of intense surprise:

> 'Oh', diss'io lui, 'or se' tu ancor morto?'   121

Surely, you're not dead? And Alberigo volunteers the information that Tolomea has a special perquisite:

> 'Cotal vantaggio ha questa Tolomea,
>   che spesse volte l'anima ci cade
>   innanzi ch'Atropòs mossa le dea.'   124-6

As a man acts treacherously in this life, his soul is instantly damned, a demon takes over the body to complete the life-span. To make his information even more credible, Alberigo mentions that Branca Doria is close by. With his nephew, Branca Doria is condemned to Tolomea for murdering his father-in-law, Michel Zanche, who was guest-of-honour at a banquet. Branca and his nephew had reached their icy fate here even before their victim Michel Zanche has reached his place among the barrators (*Inferno* xxii) so instantaneous was the punishment of such treachery. Dante is incredulous:

> ché Branca Doria non morí unquanche,
> e mangia e bee e dorme e veste panni.   140-1

Branca Doria is far from dead, but eats and drinks and sleeps and puts on clothes. Physically his body is alive and active, but the spirit within is that of a demon. In this typically medieval dichotomy of soul and body, the one possessed by the devil, the other damned in hell, there is an illustration of how strong the belief was in possession by the devil. But Dante takes it a lot further and the artistic effect is intense: it outstrips the inventiveness of many earlier punishments.

Dante, a paragon of orthodoxy, is quite unorthodox in suggesting the damnation of the living. The Christian believes that until the final moment of earthly existence he can repent. Dante himself shows how a change of heart expressed by the shedding of "una lacrimetta" (*Purg.*v.107) can win salvation for the hardened sinner. It is a comfortable belief, if one could time it accurately, but in Tolomea, Dante rules out the possibility of final repentance. The orthodox Dante throws caution to the winds and presents a central Italy inhabited not by men but by demons. It is not *un* but "il diavolo" (145), the force of evil, that takes possession of the body. What Dante has seen, what he has heard in Hell, what he has experienced at the hands of men, all confirms him in his belief that those who surround him on earth cannot be, nor have they been, men; they are men-devils, inhabiting that fair land of the mellifluous language, the "bel paese là dove 'l sí suona" (*Inf.*xxxiii.80). This apocalyptic vision may have been inspired by Psalm 54:16, "let them go down alive into hell", and by John 13:27, "and after the morsel, Satan entered into him", so that Dante had the authority he needed for the extravagance of the suggestion. It is interesting to reflect that the gospel reference is to Satan entering the body of Judas and in the next canto one of the sinners chewed by Lucifer is in fact Judas himself. A comparison with such sources, however, shows that Dante made the idea very much his own. With this image, contact with the damned ends. Alberigo is the last one to whom Dante speaks. He is now close to Lucifer and in such an atmosphere of congealment, of no life, of no humanity, of terrifying sin, the artistic conclusion, if not the logical or theological one, is that society is not a concourse of men, but of demons.

Before returning to Ugolino, consider why Dante deceives Alberigo. He does not remove the ice from his eyes: "e io non gliel' apersi" (149). His comment on this action is: "e cortesia fu lui esser villano" (150), where Dante starkly contrasts the two terms *cortesia* and *villania*, which in medieval tradition had a precise antithetical semantic value. On the human level this prompts the same reaction as in the encounter with Bocca degli Abati. Dante's action seems to be inhuman particularly as it is at the expense of a helpless and suffering subject. But to Dante, the judge and minister of God, Alberigo and Bocca are sinners who rejected goodness and chose cruelty. He sees in them the reality of sin, without any extenuating features. Dante is seeking God – the *Commedia* is an *itinerarium mentis in Deum*[6] – and there is no God in these sinners. The inscription on the door of Hell told us that the dungeon of sin was created by the justice of God. If Dante were to relieve the pain of Alberigo he would offend divine justice. So his act is churlish on the human level, but respectful of the law of God on the divine level. Dante's role as pilgrim is to acquire full knowledge of evil, so that, recognising it for what it is, he can reject it and repent. Virgil is leading Dante through Hell so that he can acquire "esperïenza piena" (*Inf.*xxviii.48), and we must associate ourselves with Dante in this role and remember his statement in the epistle to Can Grande that the practical didactic intention of his *Commedia* is "to remove those living in this life from a state of misery, and to bring them to a state of happiness".[7]

Only by such an approach can episodes such as the ones of Bocca degli Abati or Frate Alberigo be understood. They are initially perplexing for the reader, who, because the world is too much with us, tends to identify closely with the former human condition of the sinners and finds it difficult to acquire the necessary detachment. Pier della Vigna said "uomini fummo"(*Inf.*xiii.37), but now they are no longer men, nor must they be regarded as men in an active situation. The condition of damnation is static and is not imposed on them from without. They accuse themselves of their sin, "l'anima mal nata ... tutta si confessa" (*Inf.*v.7-8), and they go of their own will to their place of punishment:

> le fa di trapassar parer sí pronte   *Inf.*iii.74

> Come d'autunno si levan le foglie
>   l'una appresso de l'altra, fin che 'l ramo
>   vede a la terra tutte le sue spoglie,
> similemente il mal seme d'Adamo
>   gittansi di quel lito ad una ad una,
>   per cenni come augel per suo richiamo.   *Inf.*iii.112-17

> . . . la divina giustizia li sprona,
>   sí che la tema si volve in disio.   *Inf.*iii.125-6

To return to Ugolino: it is a tribute to Dante's genius that in this atmosphere of inhumanity, in the gradually intensified alienation from humanity that has been developed here in the frozen lake of Hell, he has placed the most humanly moving episode of the *Commedia.* In this lake of eternal hatred he gives expression to the greatest love. The tears of the sinners have frozen to block their eye sockets:

> Lo pianto stesso lí pianger non lascia,
>   e 'l duol che truova in su li occhi rintoppo,
>   si volge in entro a far crescer l'ambascia.   94-6

In this complete seizing up of human emotion there is a story, the longest single narrative in the *Commedia,* that is deliberately created to move us to tears. Ugolino asks what can make his listener weep if not his tale: "e se non piangi, di che pianger suoli?" (42).

Dante's detachment in presenting Ugolino and Ruggieri and the abrupt ending to *Inferno* xxxii, creating a deliberate break between the setting of the story and the story itself, have already been remarked upon. Now consider the first line of *Inferno* xxxiii: "La bocca sollevò dal fiero pasto". The operative word is "sollevò". It draws attention to a cessation, to a suspension of the eternal condition of the damned one. Ugolino stops his gnawing, he wipes his mouth, a deliberate gesture of withdrawal from Ruggieri, and then begins: "Poi cominciò" (4). Marcazzan has drawn attention to two echoes in this initial *terzina* of *Inferno* xxxiii that are relevant to a reading of the canto in *chiave politica*, which is, in part, being attempted here.[8] He suggests that the "fiero pasto" recalls Farinata's "fieramente furo avversi a me" (*Inf.*x.46-7) and that "forbendola" recalls Brunetto Latini's admonition to Dante "dai lor costumi fa che tu ti forbi" (*Inf.*xv.69). In both cases the earlier dialogues were centred on the ferocity of political conditions, on the anguish of exile and on the necessity of rising above factional feeling that only results in bloodshed.

There are also a number of points of similarity between this episode and that of Francesca in *Inferno* v, and one of them is precisely the element of the temporal entering into the timelessness of the punishment. Francesca and Paolo leave the troop in which Dido is placed so that they can speak to Dante. In the same way, with Ugolino, there is a temporary cessation of part of his punishment. For the gnawing of Ruggieri's skull and its contents is not just a punishment of Ruggieri, it is a punishment of Ugolino also. In the action of eating for all eternity, in the action of seeming to satisfy his hunger, there is the perennial reminder that the immediate cause of his death was starvation, but the real cause of it was hunger for political power, an unbridled form of *cupiditas,* to satisfy which he brought death on his innocent children, Dante's primary concern in the story. His very proximity to Ruggieri is also a form of punishment: for all eternity he will have as his neighbour the man whom, literally, was his deadliest enemy, the man whom he betrayed and by whom he was betrayed.

Ugolino states that he will renew his desperate grief:

> . . . 'Tu vuo' ch'io rinovelli
> disperato dolor che 'l cor mi preme

già pur pensando, pria ch'io ne favelli.'   4-6

He will at line 8, like Francesca, shed tears and words, provided
that this will bring shame to the traitor he gnaws,

'che frutti infamia al traditor ch'i' rodo,'   8

a sentiment that matches the malignant intent to hurt in Vanni
Fucci's

'e detto l'ho perché doler ti debbia!'   *Inf*.xxiv.151

Ugolino does not know who Dante is, neither does he know
how he comes to be in Antenora, nor does he care. It is
sufficient that Dante is a Florentine. This he presumably
recognises from Dante's speech, as Farinata had done
(*Inf*.x.22). Dante, therefore, must know who Ugolino and
Ruggieri were and what were their political interests. The death
of Ugolino had taken place as recently as 1289. Details of
political struggles were common knowledge to someone like
Dante as he was so involved in politics himself. In lines 13 and
14 Ugolino says that he was Count Ugolino, but the inert mass
beneath his gnawing is Archbishop Ruggieri. The difference of
tense emphasizes perhaps that Ugolino is conscious of the
futility of his human position. To others he was a count, to
himself he is the man who, so blinded by ambition, so hungry
for power, became a traitor, thus bringing a justifiable death on
his own guilty head, but an unjustified one on the innocent
heads of his children. All that is past. But Ruggieri, now both
victim and, by his very presence, punisher of the Count, is and
always will be, the man who killed him.

Ugolino does not delay in giving background details. Both
he and Ruggieri betrayed, both of them are damned. It is of the
cruelty of his death, "come la morte mia fu cruda" (20), of its
rawness that Ugolino will speak. He is not questioning the fact
that Ruggieri killed him, that is one of the rules of the game,
but the cruelty involved is what is condemned.

Ugolino begins his story *in medias res*. He and his children were imprisoned in a tower,

>   . . . 'la Muda
> la qual per me ha 'l titol de la fame.'   22-3

A *muda* or mew is a dark place in which it was customary to enclose hawks in order to break their spirit with fasting and weaken them through lack of air and light and sun. It does not take a flight of the imagination to equate the hawk, a rapacious bird, with Count Ugolino himself. The entire narrative abounds in images taken from the animal world and this establishes a link on the textual level with the earlier section and the following one. The ominous statement, "e che conviene ancor ch'altrui si chiuda" (24), implies that Ugolino and his children will not be the last to be starved to death in that tower. The cruelty of man to man will continue into the future. After several months, counted by the prisoners at each full moon, a dream reveals to them that their death is imminent. It is a dream at dawn just before wakening and medieval belief had it that these dreams revealed the future.[9] The very fact that the future is revealed is merciless. An old English proverb says that the angel of mercy weaves the veil that hides the future from us.

The dream is an allegory of contemporary political life, of the horrible events caused by ambition and hatred, events that reach a desperate and absurd ferocity. The reference at line 30 to the mountain that blocks the view of Lucca from the people of Pisa, "per che i Pisan veder Lucca non ponno", has the deeper meaning of great enmity and warfare separating the two communities.[10] In the dream, Ugolino and his children are the wolf and cubs, not by any means domestic animals; Ruggieri is the master of the hunt and his supporters, Gualandi, Sismondi and Lanfranchi, are the hounds: "cagne magre, studiose e conte" (31), hounds lean, trained and eager, denoted by the pejorative feminine form.

At line 35 the image of the wolf and cubs changes to that of
father and children. When tired, they are assaulted and torn to
pieces by the dogs. Ugolino's children weep in their sleep,
"pianger senti' fra 'l sonno i miei figliuoli" (38), and cry out for
bread. And the father breaks his narrative with an exclamation
to his listener: "Ben se' crudel, se tu già non ti duoli" (40). Is he
so cruel that he is not weeping? Surely he realizes what fate is
imminent? They are awake, awaiting their food. Each one has
had the dream and the possible interpretation becomes a
reality. They hear the door being nailed, "e io senti' chiavar
l'uscio di sotto" (46), as "chiavar" does not mean to lock but to
nail from the Latin *clavus*, nail. It is part of the refinement of
Ruggieri's cruelty, Ramat has noted, that the door was nailed
at the hour the food was due.[11] There is a building-up of silence,
meaningful looks, tension. Ugolino's "impetrai" (49), I turned
to stone, brings us beyond the immediate meaning, it does not
apply to him alone, it is symbolical of the hardening of all
men's hearts. The children weep and young Anselmo,
designated by the diminutive "Anselmuccio" and the "mio"
placed after for emphasis, asks why there is a look of terror on
his father's face. He knows why, but he refuses to believe it.

Time passes slowly in this tower of death. They are aware of
the sun rising in that world they know they will never see again.
The frustration and deep sorrow of the father are expressed in
his futile angry gesture of biting his hands, and the children,
misunderstanding the gesture, offer him that flesh that came
from him,

'tu ne vestisti
queste misere carni, e tu le spoglia,'   62-3

you clothed us with this wretched flesh, strip us of it. Thus is the
bond between father and son expressed by Dante. Ugolino
controls himself, for their sake, and the chilling silence
descends on all five. Once again he interrupts the narrative with
an exclamatory appeal to the earth: why did it not open and

swallow them into its bowels? "ahi dura terra, perché non t'apristi?" (66). The fourth day comes and Gaddo, after one last desperate cry consuming his final energy, falls dead at his father's feet. One by one, slowly and relentlessly, the other three die over the fifth and sixth days. Ugolino is being tortured to the utmost for what he has caused to happen to his children. Finally, blinded by hunger, he cries out their names, giving vent to the pent up anguish that, for their sakes, he had suppressed, and hunger does what sorrow had been unable to do: it kills him.

The line, "poscia, piú che 'l dolor, poté 'l digiuno" (75), has been much discussed as there seems to have been a medieval version of the story that implied that Ugolino was so blinded by hunger that he ate his own children when they were dead. There is no justification in the text for this. The line means precisely what it clearly says, a man cannot die of a broken heart, but he can die of hunger. Deeper and sinister implications have been seen by some critics, perhaps misled by De Sanctis, who follows his clear statement that "il dolore non poté ucciderlo; lo uccise la fame", by the more ambiguous one, "ma è verso fitto di tenebre e pieno di sottintesi."[12] It is rather extraordinary that the *tesi della tecnofagia* has been supported in a reading as recently as 1953.[13] It may be justified only in the light of Croce's comment that "ognuno ha diritto a dir la sua".

Ugolino had interrupted his "bestial segno" (*Inf.* xxxii.133) to speak of the bestiality of men; now that he has told his story he returns to his victim. The tale has come full circle and in the initial and final image of Ugolino there is a reversal of his role in the story. Ruggieri is no longer the master of the hunt, he is reduced to eternal immobility. Ugolino is now the dog with the sharp fangs who attempts for all eternity to satisfy the hunger, both real and symbolical, that killed him.

The appeal of Ugolino had been to tears: "e se non piangi, di che pianger suoli?" (42). Dante does not weep, rather he cries out with biblical fury for another unnatural event to match that which has just been recounted. He wills Capraia and Gorgona, two small islands in the Tyrrhenian Sea, to block the mouth of the Arno, so that it will flood and drown all the citizens of Pisa (82-4). If indeed the reader weeps, what should be the motivation of his tears?

Too often the canto has been read, quite erroneously, as one designed to evoke pity for Ugolino. De Sanctis gave the lead with his *lettura magistrale* when he wrote: "gli è che qui Ugolino non è il traditore, ma il tradito".[14] Although De Sanctis continued to qualify his statement somewhat, his attitude to Ugolino has been accepted in readings for many generations and only recently have critics adverted fully to the fact that Ugolino is "tradito" because a "traditore". It is the inexorable justice of the law of men that only those are betrayed who have betrayed. Dante condemns Ugolino totally, firstly as a traitor, hence his place in Antenora, and secondly as the real killer of his children. Of the four persons starved to death with Ugolino only two were in fact his sons, Gaddo and Uguiccione; the other two were grandsons and they were not children, as the story implies, but adults. It was quite possible that Dante did not know these details. It is also possible that he did and that he deliberately changed them in order to reinforce a point already made in *Inferno* x, when he spoke to Farinata. There, he condemned the involvement of innocent beings in political vendettas. Farinata asks Dante why the people of Florence are constantly pitiless against his kindred in all their laws. Why involve his descendants in his deeds of blood? He prophesies Dante's exile and the obvious implication is that what is happening to Farinata's descendants will happen to Dante's own. What causes Dante great sorrow in his encounter with Farinata is the awareness that he will not be alone in paying for what he has done, but his descendants will suffer also.[15] When earlier the Florentine Mosca dei Lamberti comments that his evil advice brought political strife to the city of Florence, Dante adds that it brought death to Mosca's family: "e morte di tua schiatta" (*Inf.*xxviii.109).

This is precisely Ugolino's case as presented in the story.

Dante had four children and Ugolino's four children in the story were killed with him although they had done nothing. They were innocent, as Dante reminds the city of Pisa; their very youth was sufficient reason to spare them what is called a crucifixion:

'non dovei tu i figliuoi porre a tal croce,'   87

but they were not spared, because their father was a traitor and the sins of the fathers are visited on the children. This was the law of Dante's times and of the society to which he belonged, a society that throughout the *Inferno* he condemns. In *Inferno* xxxiii Dante cries out against the Pisans, may they be drowned:

muovasi la Capraia e la Gorgona,
    e faccian siepe ad Arno in su la foce,
    sí ch'elli annieghi in te ogni persona!   82-4

He cries out against the Genoese, may they be wiped from the face of the earth:

Ahi Genovesi, uomini diversi
    d'ogne costume e pien d'ogne magagna,
    perché non siete voi del mondo spersi?   151-3

There have been other invectives in the *Inferno:* against Pistoia, the Romagna, against all of central Italy, where ambition is totally ruthless and violence is rampant. Perhaps most condemned is Florence, Dante's own city, a city which with its new people and sudden gains, "la gente nuova e i sùbiti guadagni" (*Inf.*xvi.73), has become the centre of universal perversion, where the imperial majesty is being opposed.[16] It is the city that produced the florin that makes the pastors of the people deviate from the God-given role:

. . . 'il maladetto fiore
c'ha disviate le pecore e li agni,
però che fatto ha lupo del pastore.'   *Par*.ix.130-2

Repeatedly and consistently, Dante's message throughout the
Commedia is that the natural order of Emperor and Pope
guiding man in his terrestrial life is being rejected.

No one escapes Dante's fierce whip. He condemns and
damns not just those opposed to him as one might expect;
Dante damned both Guelph and Ghibelline, both the Neri
party and the Bianchi party, both personal friend and personal
enemy. He condemned his own society, a society of men such
as he was, men inflamed like him with the fire of party passion,
men lost in a "selva oscura" where ambition was called
patriotism, vicious attack seen as self-defence and unbridled
cruelty as just punishment. The tragedy of paternal love in
Ugolino, in Farinata (so concerned for "i miei"), in Dante, was
brought about by political conditions, but Dante, Ugolino and
Farinata were guilty parties in the creation of these same
political conditions. The bond of father and son is nature's
deepest: "tu ne vestisti queste misere carni" (62-3). Yet these
men could break the bond of nature, and they are so blinded by
cupiditas, that they involve their innocent children in their
deeds of blood. They are the betrayers and the betrayed, they
are the makers of their own personal hell, they are the activists,
the creators of the political conditions of which inexorably
they are also victims.

What Dante condemns is the inhumanity of man to man. In
Inferno xxxiii we find the unequivocal statement that demonic
forces have taken possession of men and there is an apocalyptic
final image of an Italy populated by demons. This ends the
canto. The last canto of the *Inferno* is xxxiv and it presents
Lucifer, "la creatura ch'ebbe il bel sembiante" (*Inf*.xxxiv.18),
who, once so fair, was the being created like man unto the
image of God, an image that both he and men rejected.

Notes

[1]Other stages in the development of this theme are his encounters with Farinata and Cavalcante, Pier della Vigna, Brunetto Latini, Iacopo Rusticcucci and his Florentine companions, Frate Gomita and Michel Zanche, Vanni Fucci, Guido da Montefeltro, Mosca dei Lamberti, Geri del Bello (against whom Dante failed to carry out the obligatory vendetta). The theme finally reaches a climax of apocalyptic proportions and demonic force in the exchanges between Dante on the one hand and Bocca degli Abati, Ugolino and Ruggieri, Frate Alberigo and Branca Doria, on the other.

[2]"Il Conte Ugolino", *Cultura e scuola,* 13-14 (1965), 518-27 (p. 520), by R. Ramat, as he interprets the episode in a modern historical perspective, marks an important move away from a tradition greatly influenced by De Sanctis. It is difficult to accept Mario Sansone's criticism of it, especially as Sansone's own valuable reading is in the same key. See M. Sansone, "Il canto XXXIII dell'*Inferno*", *Nuove letture dantesche* (Florence, 1966—), III (1969), 143-87.

[3]See T. S. Eliot, "Hamlet and his Problems", *The Sacred Wood,* second edition (London, 1928), p. 100.

[4]P. McNair, "The Poetry of the *Comedy*", in *The Mind of Dante*, ed. U. Limentani (Cambridge, 1965), pp. 17-46 (p. 18).

[5]E. Moore, *Studies in Dante,* first series reprinted (Oxford, 1969), p. 248.

[6]C. S. Singleton, *Dante Studies 2: Journey to Beatrice,* second edition (Cambridge, Mass., 1967), p. 5.

[7]*Dantis Alagherii epistolae: The Letters of Dante*, ed. Paget Toynbee, second edition (Oxford, 1966), p. 178: " . . . quod finis totius et partis est, removere viventes in hac vita de statu miseriae, et perducere ad statum felicitatis."

[8]M. Marcazzan, "Canto XXXIII", in *Lectura Dantis Scaligera: Inferno* (Florence, 1967), pp. 1161-96 (p. 1175).

[9]In *Inferno* xxvi.7, significantly following the invective against Florence, Dante mentions the belief in dreams at dawn: "Ma se

presso al mattin del ver si sogna". See also *Purg.*ix.16-18 and *Conv.*II.viii.13.

[10]A. Pézard, "Le Chant XXXIII de l'Enfer", *Letture dell'Inferno,* ed. V. Vettori (Milan, 1963), pp. 343-96 (p. 350).

[11]Ramat, p. 525. See note 2.

[12]F. De Sanctis, "Il canto XXXIII dell'*Inferno*" in *Letture dantesche,* ed. G. Getto, second edition, 3 vols (Florence, 1968), I, 651-71 (p.667). See also F. De Sanctis, *Saggi critici,* II (Milan, 1929).

[13]G. Raya, "Il canto di Ugolino", in *Studi in onore di S. Santangelo* (Catania, 1953).

[14]De Sanctis in *Letture dantesche,* p. 654. See note 12.

[15]This interpretation is admirably expounded by J. A. Scott in "Politics and *Inferno* X", *Italian Studies,* 19 (1964), 1-13.

[16]See Dante, "Epistola VI", "Dantes Alagherii Florentinus et exul immeritus Scelestissimis Florentinis intrinsecis", pp. 66-76 of the Toynbee edition, see note 6.

The "Maggior Fortuna" and the Siren in Purgatorio XIX

W. B. Stanford

Commentators[1] have failed to find a convincing reason for Dante's reference to the *Fortuna Major* in the lines:

> —quando i geomanti lor Maggior Fortuna
> veggiono in orïente, innanzi a l'alba,
> surger per via che poco le sta bruna — . *Purg.*xix.4-6

It is hardly sufficient to say that here the *Fortuna Major* merely marks the approach of dawn. Other stars or configurations of stars could have served that simple purpose. An unusual reference demands something more than a commonplace explanation, especially when one is dealing with an author who does not exhibit esoteric learning for exhibitionistic reasons. Besides, the mention of the geomancers suggests some kind of prediction or oracle. Paparelli speaks of "un'aura di magia e di ermetismo", but offers no more precise interpretation of the symbolism, nor does any other commentator that I have seen.

At least we know what the *Fortuna* looked like. Vernon,[2] quoting Benvenuto da Imola, and Tozer[3] describe it. It consisted of six stars in the constellations of Aquarius and Pisces forming the pattern ✳✳✳✳. This is common knowledge. What will now be suggested is, perhaps, new. If one draws lines to join these star-dots, as the ancient astronomers regularly did to construct their spectacular picture-book of mythology in the skies, then the resulting outline, if set upright, is like the shape of a two-pronged fork or else like the letter Y with the upper arms extended vertically. The second comparison may seem rather strained. But, as is well known, Dante saw even more far-fetched letter-shapes elsewhere in his *Commedia*. In *Purgatorio* xxiii.32-3, he saw the letters O M O in the outlines of men's eyebrows, eyes and nose. In *Paradiso* xviii.75-96 he found D, I, L and other letters patterned by spirits as if in the flight of birds, to spell the words "*DILIGITE IUSTITIAM*" and "*QUI IUDICATIS TERRAM*", and then by a reverse process he identified the letter M with the head and neck of an eagle (*Par*.xviii.107-8).[4] In these references there is a significant relationship between the letter-shape and the matter in hand. Can one too find a similar relation between the letter Y and the context in *Purgatorio* xix?

The ancient Greeks and Romans, as well as several medieval writers, called the letter *upsilon* and its Latin equivalent, Y, "the Pythagorean letter".[5] A source familiar to early medieval scholars and writers was Servius's note on *Aeneid* 6, 136:

> As we know Pythagoras of Samos divided human life according to the manner of the letter Y. That is because the early period of life is in a state of uncertainty, not being decisively devoted to virtue or vice. The parting of the ways [*bivium*] of the letter Y begins after one's youth, when men follow vices, represented by the left-hand part of the letter, or virtues [that is the right-hand part].

Medieval readers would find similar references to the Pythagorean letter, also called Samian from Pythagoras's birth-place, in Persius, Ausonius, Saint Jerome, Martianus

Capella and Isidore of Seville.[6] Lactantius summarized the prevailing view tersely:[7] "They say that the course of human life is like the letter Y". In the later medieval period both Petrarch[8] and Richard de Bury[9] mention this symbolism allusively. It seems likely, then, that Dante was familiar with it.

If that is so, the purpose of the reference to the *Fortuna* could have been to introduce the notion of an ethical choice at the transition from youth to manhood. In the previous canto Dante had explored the doctrine of sensual and spiritual love and had rejected the kind of romantic love that he, as a younger man, had idealized. But he saw that without the impetus of some kind of strong love *accidia* would result, as exemplified in the laggard Jews after the crossing of the Red Sea and the Trojans who stayed behind in Sicily. Then at the end of *Purgatorio* xviii he began to dream and, at the beginning of *Purgatorio* xix, after references to Saturn (apparently as an emblem of *accidia*) and the *Fortuna Major,* the Siren appeared.

Here a further perplexity arises. The symbolism of the Siren has been discussed almost *ad nauseam*.[10] Only two aspects of it will be noticed, very briefly, here. First, the psychological origin of her introduction may be traced back to the mention of wax in *Purgatorio* xviii.39. The story of how plugs of wax were used by Ulysses to prevent his crew from hearing the Sirens' song was so well known in the medieval period[11] that any mention of wax in a literary context would probably have suggested the Sirens' song to a sophisticated writer or reader, just as in modern times a grid-iron suggests Saint Lawrence and a shamrock, Saint Patrick.

Secondly, what is the link between the Siren and the Pythagorean letter visible in the *Fortuna Major*? And who is the "donna santa e presta" in line 26, who now enters to unmask the inner hideousness of the Siren? Again the commentators have offered widely different views. Two of them, Cary, in the notes to his translation, and Hardie,[12] have cursorily mentioned a classical analogy that may give the right clue: the Choice of Hercules,[13] although they may have found it in older commentaries. For this was a commonplace in classical literature from the fourth century onwards, its earliest appearance being in Xenophon's *Memorabilia* (2, 1, 21 ff.), where the allegory is attributed to Prodicus the Sophist. The story was that Hercules as a young man came to a fork in a road, the road of life. There two women confronted him, each trying to persuade him to choose her way. One, of course, personified virtue, the other, vice. Perhaps the Siren and the appearance of "una donna santa e presta", one set off against the other, emblemize the same kind of decision here.

There are two main objections to this interpretation. The first is theological, that it implies too humanistic an attitude towards moral choice. This could be argued for ever without a clear verdict. The second objection once seemed to be more conclusive. It was authoritatively stated that the Choice of Hercules was not referred to in the medieval period until Coluccio Salutati's treatise *De laboribus Herculis*.[14] But it has now been shown that Petrarch mentioned it twice. [15] When Petrarch could refer to it rather casually, it seems fairly probable that Dante may have known about it, too, since there was no need for familiarity with Greek sources in this case. If so, the "Maggior Fortuna" becomes clear: it symbolizes the choice that a young man must make when he comes to choose his way of life. Will he, like Ulysses, as Dante thought, be drawn from the right course by Vice masquerading as Pleasure,[16] a hideous thing when stripped of its fine clothes, or will he follow Virtue?[17]

Notes

[1] I am indebted to Mr. T. O'Neill for help with commentaries on Dante. For G. Paparelli see *Lectura Dantis Scaligera:*

Purgatorio (Florence, 1967), pp. 693-755. The *Fortuna* is mentioned by M. A. Orr, *Dante and the Early Astronomers* (London, 1956), p. 187, but not discussed.

[2]W. W. Vernon, *Readings on the "Purgatorio" of Dante,* third edition, 2 vols (London, 1907), II, 106.

[3]H. F. Tozer, *An English Commentary on Dante's "Divina Commedia"* (Oxford, 1901), p. 305.

[4]This kind of letter symbolism goes back to classical Greece, the earliest recorded example being Aeschrion's (fourth century B. C.) description of the crescent moon as "heaven's beautiful new letter sigma". For other examples see F. Dornseiff, *Das Alphabet in Mystik und Magie, Stoicheia,* vol. 7 (Leipzig, 1922), and W. B. Stanford, *Greek Metaphor* (Oxford, 1936), pp. 65-7.

[5]Theodor E. Mommsen, "Petrarch and the Story of the Choice of Hercules", *Journal of the Warburg and Courtauld Institutes,* 16 (1953), 178-92 (p. 184), has a bibliography on this. I owe many references to this article. See, too, the general essay by P. Damon, "Geryon, Cacciaguida, and the Y of Pythagoras", *Dante Studies,* 85 (1967), 15-32.

[6]The references to these authors are respectively: *Satires* 3, 56-7; *De litteris monosyllabis* (348)9; *De nuptiis* etc. 2, 102; *Espistolae* 107, 6, 3 (ed. Hilberg); *Etymol.* 1, 3, 7 (ed. Lindsay). See *Thesaurus Linguae Latinae,* ii, 2024-5, at *bivium.* For "Dante's probable use of the Commentary of Servius" see E. Moore, *Studies in Dante, first series: Scripture and Classical Authors in Dante* (Oxford, 1896), pp. 189-91. See, too, R. Hollander, *Allegory in Dante's "Commedia"* (Princeton, 1969), pp. 96-7.

[7]*Div. inst.* 6, 3, 1-2 (ed. Brandt), and 6, 3, 6 ff.

[8]*Famil.* 3, 12, 5; 7, 17, 1; 12, 3, 5-6; *Ep. metricae,* ii, p. 50, 1-15 (ed. Rossetti).

[9]*Philobiblion,* ii, 35 (ed. West).

[10]Very fully given by Paparelli as cited in note 1.

[11]For this theme and for the Siren incident in general in post-pagan literature see Hugo Rahner, *Greek Myths and Christian*

Mystery, in translation (London, 1963), pp. 328-86.

[12]Colin Hardie, "Il canto XIX", *Lectura Dantis internazionale: Letture del "Purgatorio"*, ed. V. Vettori (Milan, 1965), pp. 217-49. For Cary see *The Vision; or Hell, Purgatory, and Paradise, of Dante Alighieri,* translated by Henry Cary (London, 1840), p. 274; or any edition.

[13]Mommsen, see note 5, discusses this theme in detail, but without reference to Dante.

[14]E. Panofsky, *Hercules am Scheidewege und andere antike Bildstoffe in der neueren Kunst:* Studien der Bibliothek Warburg, 18 (Leipzig and Berlin, 1930), p. 155; cited by Mommsen p. 178, see note 5.

[15]*De vita solitaria* (begun in 1346) 1, 4, 2, and 2, 9, 4, cited by Mommsen, p. 178, see note 5. An easily accessible classical source was Cicero, *De off.* 1, 32, 118, and 3, 5, 25. Petrarch combines the notion of Hercules's choice with "the Pythagorean letter" in *De vita solitaria* 2, 9, 4: see Mommsen, pp. 182-4.

[16]For the Siren as an emblem of worldly allurements see *Purg.* xxxi.45-6 and *Epistolae* VIII, 4, according to Paparelli p. 714, see note 1, but "Epistola V", 4, in Toynbee's edition.

[17]A third consideration might be added: why is the Siren first seen as ugly and stammering, and then transformed as soon as Dante pays attention to her? Perhaps because she emblemizes, as she did for earlier Christian writers — see Rahner, pp. 361-2, as cited in note 11 — the beauty of the pagan tradition, as well as the timeless seduction of sensuality and vice. To the medieval mind that ancient tradition had been vividly painted in hideous colours by Christian apologists. But, as the men of the Renaissance would soon see, if anyone looks at that pagan tradition attentively it regains a desirable loveliness. In other words, perhaps here Dante for a moment anticipates, and rejects, the attitude of the Renaissance to the pagan Graeco-Roman tradition. A similar suggestion that Dante's presentation of Ulysses in *Inferno* xxvi implies an anticipation and rejection of the Renaissance spirit is offered in my *The*

Ulysses Theme, second edition (Oxford, 1963), pp. 178-82. See Singh's reference to this work in his commentary on *Inferno* xxvi above.

Purgatorio XXVII

P. Calì

As Giovanni Boccaccio, the first recorded lecturer on Dante's poem, remarked long ago in the *proemio* to his *Comento,* the commentator's task is " . . . spiegare l'artificioso testo, la moltitudine delle storie e la sublimità de' sensi, nascosi sotto il poetico velo della *Commedia* del nostro Dante".[1] This programme of study, outlined in Boccaccio's public readings in 1373 and 1374 in the church of Santo Stefano in Badia in Florence, has been carried out by an endless number of scholars for the last six hundred years so that a formidable body of exegetic material has accumulated in which all possible tastes and tendencies have been accommodated.

Side by side with the many commentators who have striven to draw aside the "poetico velo" of the *litera* in order to bring to light the hidden sense, a considerable number of critics have devoted their attention to the analysis and evaluation of the poetical values of the text. Sometimes the two approaches, instead of following parallel lines of development, have been sharply antithetical. In recent times there are signs that the two critical tendencies have come closer to equilibrium and

approached a synthesis, thus helping an understanding of the
poem's meaning and an appreciation of the poetry.

It is not easy in each and every canto of the *Commedia* to
grasp simultaneously poetic imagery and allegorical purpose,
literal fiction and symbolic function, dramatic representation
and doctrinal intention. Indeed a satisfactory appreciation of
both aspects may only be obtained in a comprehensive view of
the whole poem in its organic unity rather than in a single canto
or even in each single *cantica*. Yet, in spite of this, *Purgatorio*
xxvii very effectively lends itself to a unified appraisal of
imaginative power and relevant symbolism.

The canto opens with what may seem at first sight a
complex, if not abstruse, astronomical periphrasis with which
the poet describes the hour of sunset on the mountain of
Purgatory:

> Sí, come quando i primi raggi vibra
>   là dove il suo fattor lo sangue sparse,
>   cadendo Ibero sotto l'alta Libra,
> e l'onde in Gange da nona rïarse,
>   sí stava il sole; onde 'l giorno sen giva,
>   come l'angel di Dio lieto ci apparse.   1-6

When, however, the reader, with the help of an explanatory
note, has made out the position of the sun in the sky by which,
according to Dante's cosmography, it is dawn in Jerusalem,
midnight in Spain, midday in India, he will realize that, while
the light is fading on the horizon of Purgatory, the poet has
traced out, as it were, an imaginary cross, whose arms, running
from north to south and from east to west, seem to embrace the
whole earth. The present tense of "vibra" in the first line,
followed by the ablative absolute "cadendo" in the third,
together with an *essendo* to be understood in the fourth,
convey a sensation of the steady flow of time, the ceaseless
succession of day and night brought about by the motion of the
sun. But the vibration of the sun's rays is both physical and

spiritual, falling as they do on the place where the central event of Christian history and therefore of Dante's history took place, Christ's sacrifice, the event by which the Creator, "fattor", became Redeemer, and contact was made between the human and the divine through grace, whose permanent, illuminating symbol, the sun is, as indicated in the first hemistich of line 5 by "stava".

Until now the *Purgatorio* has been punctuated by frequent astronomical periphrases marking the passage of time and scanning the various stages of the pilgrim's moral progress. But never before has a geographical indication been charged so densely and so emblematically with a sense of the sacred. Every spatial and temporal component is perceived in a vast synchronization of symbolic nature which sets the poetic tone of the canto. Noon over the Ganges coincides with the liturgical hour of nones on Mount Purgatory and the appropriate atmosphere is obviously being developed here for a crucial moment of the ascent. The third day spent in Purgatory is at hand and will mark the conclusion of the expiatory process which Christ's sacrifice made possible.

There is a slight tinge of melancholy in the second half of line 5, "onde 'l giorno sen giva", in which the prolonged sound and rhythm convey the fall of evening and the resumption of the way and seem to echo "lo giorno se n'andava" (*Inf.*ii.1) at the beginning of the fateful journey. Here, however, there is no sense of gloom and whatever feeling of sadness there may be is mitigated by, and indeed, vanishes with that "lieto", the gladness of God's angel, welcoming with joyful notes the pilgrim and his companions, Virgil and Statius, about to leave the last terrace where lust is purged:

> Fuor de la fiamma stava in su la riva,
> 　e cantava '*Beati mundo corde!*'
> 　in voce assai piú che la nostra viva.　　　　7-9

The angel of chastity standing on the terrace on the outer edge which the flames do not reach, unlike some of the previous heavenly creatures who presided over each turning-point of the purgatorial climb, is a featureless figure and yet his presence, so wholly transcendental, so concretely expressed with "stava" (the same verb that two lines earlier had marked the presence of the sun), is fully achieved through the intensity of his singing voice. Line 8 with the dominance of long, open vowels offers a pure *a solo,* hovering above flame and rock to proclaim in the simple melody of plain chant the blessedness of the pure in heart.

More than being an important feature of the poem's structural symmetry, the beatitudes within Purgatory proper always strike a musical chord which resounds as an insistent, cheerful invitation to advance further and higher.[2] Here, however, the pure line of verbal melody is suddenly interrupted by the announcement on the part of the angel of the fixed norm of this uppermost terrace:

> Poscia 'Piú non si va, se pria non morde,
>   anime sante, il foco: intrate in esso,
>   e al cantar di là non siate sorde',
> ci disse come noi li fummo presso.   10-13

This injunction is delivered with a tranquil yet firm tone somewhat softened by the brotherly vocative "anime sante" and by the encouragement to the wayfarers to proceed confidently to another penitential act, a ritual purification through which they will be led by a mysteriously alluring song that is full of promise.

The implicit acceptance by Virgil and Statius, who already belong to the world of the supernatural, forms a contrast to Dante's reaction of paralysing terror, natural enough in a man who is still carrying "quel d'Adamo" (*Purg.*ix.10). Straightaway the imagination conjures up horrifying ways of dying. He is seized by fear like a human being condemned to die by *propagginazione* (15), the fate of the assassin planted head down in a hole, which is then filled with earth so that he eventually suffocates.[3] The inner terror is then transferred into the dramatic gesture of the following *terzina*, "una delle più belle del poema" according to Niccolò Tommaseo:

> In su le man commesse mi protesi,
> guardando il foco e imaginando forte
> umani corpi già veduti accesi. 16-18

Whatever the exact interpretation of line 16,[4] the impact of the *terzina* is strong because of Dante's realistic gesture of exorcism and the intensity of his looking at the flames.

It is a highly distressing situation and Virgil, tacitly supported by Statius, intervenes promptly with all his loving care and moral authority and even appeals to the supernatural power which has enabled him to guide and assist his charge so far. But no appeal to filial devotion, however affectionate in the anxious "Figliuol mio" at the end of line 20, no argument however persuasive can move Dante; no assurance about the nature of the fire which can purify but cannot consume, no exhortation can cause Dante to budge, even when Virgil, seeming to gesticulate, eloquently insists:

> 'fatti ver' lei, e fatti far credenza', 29

> 'pon giú omai, pon giú ogne temenza;
> volgiti in qua e vieni: entra sicuro!' 31-2

His bodily fear remains stronger than the dictates of his reason and moral conscience.

The whole sequence is highly dramatic and credibly realistic. From a structural viewpoint this scene represents the development of the theme of fire from *Purgatorio* xxv and xxvi where Dante saw the expiation of lust and its deviations and heard the praise of chastity. Now the fire assumes a wider dimension. Besides being the penance of the seventh terrace it forms the wall of flames surrounding the mountain-top through which all souls must pass in order to reach the earthly paradise, perhaps that is the biblical *gladius flammeus* of the cherub guarding the place and enacting divine justice, a comprehensive sign of ritual discipline "quasi di compendio ed estremo simbolo di tutto il processo di purificazione" (a summation almost and ultimate symbol of the whole process of purification).[5] Popular imagination after all, in the Middle Ages associated purgatorial penance mainly with fire. And not only in medieval times. One recalls Manzoni's description of the country shrine on Don Abbondio's path: "on which were painted long, snaky shapes with pointed ends, supposed, in the mind of the artist and to the eyes of the local inhabitants, to represent flames; alternating with the flames were other shapes defying description, and these were meant to be souls in Purgatory."[6] There was a vast amount of theological writing on the purifying function of fire based on the Scriptures and elaborated by the Church Fathers. Pazzaglia in a recent commentary on this canto has diligently gathered together the most significant examples from Paul to Ambrose, from Augustine to Bonaventure, together with the numerous indications by previous commentators on Dante.[7]

By attending, however, to the literal narrative, in which poetry communicates more directly, it is clear that the poet has developed more and more the motif of terror caused by the flames from the initial description of the fire and its dangerous proximity, "e io temea il foco" (*Purg*.xxv.111-16), to his sighting of Guinizelli,

rimirando lui,
né, per lo foco, in là piú m'appressai,   *Purg*.xxvi.101-2

until the critical point is now reached in *Purgatorio* xxvii. The pilgrim, all along the narrow edge, has been skirting the fire,

flinching from it, now he must face it. The physical terror
which immobilizes him, however, is not enough to explain his
stubborn resistance, as Ulrich Leo suggested in his analysis of
the passage. In his opinion this "è, se mai, la paura del cattolico
credente, che ancora sulla terra si raffigura in forma concreta il
fuoco del Purgatorio; non l'avventura dell'anima, penitente ma
già salvata, che in esso sarà purificata."[8]

But this is a half-truth as, in fact, one of the most crucial
moments of the *avventura dell'anima* now confronts the
reader. The word "coscïenza" in line 33 intimates an inner
struggle taking place at the very core of the pilgrim's psyche, a
struggle that the *lumen naturale* cannot solve. The reference in:

> Ricorditi, ricorditi! E se io
>   sovresso Gerïon ti guidai salvo, 22-3

to the Geryon flight in *Inferno* xvii is illuminating. Faced in
Geryon with the personification of fraud, natural reason was
able to defend the pilgrim from the sting of the monster's
poisonous tail and, consequently, to guide him through the
foul world of Malebolge, plumbing the depth of an evil that yet
never engulfed him as he was kept apart from it. Now the same
faculty of reason seems incapable of overcoming a
predicament more subtle than the resistance of the senses.

Dante here is called upon to submit himself to a process of
purification not only of the excesses of the flesh but also of all
those impulses of the spirit which tend to deify human love,
that ambiguous mixture of Christian idealism and eroticism
which courtly love poetry had often exalted and whose impure
component Guinizelli and Arnaut are here expiating in the
refining flame. He must abandon the equating of gentleness,
beauty and virtue with passion, an equation which placed
Francesca in the first circle. The necessity of discarding this
fascinating but mistaken form of love is represented as an
excruciating experience to shake Dante the man and the poet
to the very foundation of his being. In order to eradicate all

extremes of lust from the body and from the soul Dante must go, body and soul, through the fire which will burn the dross, but at one and the same time rekindle in him another flame. Fire must be fought with fire, a lower form of love must be absorbed into a higher form of love. No rationalizing power can transform in this way. The only way is the way of the heart:

> Quando mi vide star pur fermo e duro,
>   turbato un poco disse: 'Or vedi, figlio:
>   tra Bëatrice e te è questo muro'.
> Come al nome di Tisbe aperse il ciglio
>   Piramo in su la morte, e riguardolla,
>   allor che 'l gelso diventò vermiglio;
> cosí, la mia durezza fatta solla,
>   mi volsi al savio duca, udendo il nome
>   che ne la mente sempre mi rampolla.   34-42

Poetically, the reference in a simile to the Ovidian treatment of the myth of Pyramus and Thisbe, glimpsed at the culminating moment of the pathetic fusion of love and death, serves to relax the tension of the drama into a feeling of tender intimacy. Certainly at first sight one can hardly see that there is a perfect correspondence between the two emotional situations, especially if one considers the circumstances surrounding the legend of the two young lovers of Babylon. Nevertheless the episode of the mythical lover's reanimation works effectively as an objective correlative.[9] Just as Thisbe's passionate uttering of her name over the dying Pyramus could revive him, so, miraculously, the mere mention of Beatrice's name arouses in Dante a new energy. But the analogy goes deeper than that as it suggests a degree of contrast. Whereas love, however intense, could suspend Pyramus's death for a brief while only, Beatrice's love invests Dante's mind with a power that would conquer death itself, reawakening in him a new life which is destined to endure and regenerate itself like spring water, as is so wonderfully suggested by the meaning "gushes forth continuously" of "rampolla" (42). It seems hardly necessary to extend the meaning of Pyramus's blood, reddening the mulberry tree at line 39, to make it a symbol of Christ's blood staining the cross, as suggested by some medieval allegories of the Ovidian text, in order to establish here the relevance of the Christian paradox that "to live one has to die". Nor is it necessary to follow Pietro di Dante to the other end of the interpretative spectrum when he says that the same line "figurat deflorationem virginis puellae", a vice to which, in his opinion, the *auctor* was rather prone.[10] Yet the idyllic character of the poetic fable reverberates in the scene in such a way as to suggest the romantic atmosphere which surrounded the story of Dante's love for Beatrice as told in the *Vita Nuova*. The pursuit of pure love represented by Beatrice in the youthful romance had been marred by or confused with sentimental distractions whose unworthiness now comes to the surface in the poet's consciousness. Soon they also will be burned away. Consequently it is at this point that, over and above the idealism of the *Vita Nuova*, Beatrice begins to enter truly and effectively upon her role as guide to God's love.

The inner drama having been resolved, the narrative now at last leads us speedily and confidently through the fire to a new beginning. The ritual *transitus per ignem*, a tremendous ordeal that is a sacramental act by which the old man is destroyed and simultaneously the new man is born, is condensed most economically into a few lines of hyperbolic intensity, marked by a strong accentuation which reminds us of some typical Dantean verse that described the pains of Hell:

> Sí com' fui dentro, in un bogliente vetro
>   gittato mi sarei per rinfrescarmi,
>   tant' era ivi lo 'ncendio sanza metro.   49-51

The passage through the fire is quick, once again led by Virgil smiling paternally, tantalizingly, almost humorously, before preceding Dante into the flames:

'Come!
volenci star di qua?'; indi sorrise
come al fanciul si fa ch'è vinto al pome.   43-5

Beatrice's eyes are there too, consoling and inviting, but it is the music, again a liturgical chant, which leads, first distant then clear, with the most blissful of welcomes: *"Venite, benedicti Patris mei"* (58), Christ's own words resounding from within a blinding light. In a fine, chiaroscuro contrast with the angel's brightness, echoing a similar moment in the earlier part of the canto, the motif of the day's ending returns here, marked this time by an unmistakably spiritual resonance:

'Lo sol sen va', soggiunse, 'e vien la sera;
non v'arrestate, ma studiate il passo,
mentre che l'occidente non si annera,'   61-3

clearly a paraphrase of John 12.35: "Ambulate dum lucem habetis ne tenebrae vos comprehendant".
   The renewed impulse to ascend is thwarted, according to the law of the mountain, by the fall of darkness and on the steps of the stairway the three wayfarers make their beds on stone.

E pria che 'n tutte le sue parti immense
fosse orizzonte fatto d'uno aspetto,
e notte avesse tutte sue dispense,
ciascun di noi d'un grado fece letto;
ché la natura del monte ci affranse
la possa del salir piú e 'l diletto.   70-5

The *Purgatorio* abounds in lyrical passages describing the beauty of nature, of alternating day and night which constantly accompany with their symbolic presence the vicissitudes of the journey of renewal. As at the beginning of the canto, once more the traveller is presented with an earthly landscape and a time of day pregnant with spiritual meaning. Three lonely creatures,

three human destinies, isolated on a stair hewn out of the bare
rock, on the last stair which looks to the east from where the
sun's light, emblem of salvation, will rise again. Meanwhile the
shadows gather slowly all around from the farthest corners of
the horizon until the whole vast expanse is immersed in
darkness and silence suggesting so closely the presence of the
infinite where the spirit can feel God.

And so the last day in Purgatory has come to an end. A
meditative mood now sets in, appropriately enough for the
climbers as they prepare to bivouac. But it is introduced by
what may at first sight appear a somewhat inappropriate and
long-drawn-out simile consisting of two complementary
images. Dante compares himself to a goat and the guides to
shepherds, "io come capra, ed ei come pastori" (86), at the end
of the similes that describe goats ruminating in the hot
afternoon after ranging freely to graze on the hill-tops, guarded
by the shepherd. Then, transposing and extending the image,
the herdsman is described spending the night in the open,
watching his flock to protect them against wild beasts (76-87).
As modern commentators like Momigliano and Sapegno
agree, it is not a bucolic scene but, apart from sensing in it a
solemn scenario of biblical resonance where silence introduces
communion with nature and with God, they see no symbolic
significance in this pastoral interlude, although they do not
exclude it. Mario Pazzaglia refers to the medieval bestiaries
and biblical commentaries in which the goat, with its sharp
sight and love of high peaks, represented in a tropological sense
the virtue of prophecy or the disposition to contemplation and
in which it was even seen as representing Christ.[11]

On the other hand Rocco Montano interprets the goats here
as the herd of instincts or temptations, all the wrong impulses
which the pilgrim has mastered with the help of reason and
science, under the control of which they must be continually
watched.[12] The latter seems to be a plausible interpretation in
view of the fact that the poet links, by repetition, the goats'
"ruminando" in line 76 with the pilgrim's "ruminando" in line

91. But the two interpretations are not mutually exclusive and they may actually coalesce into an acceptable ambivalence of symbolic meaning. The pilgrim, while mulling over his past recklessness and wantonness, having gone through a cathartic experience, now feels the urge to direct all the potentialities of his being towards the higher regions of the spiritual life. Recollecting past dissipations. man in his inner awareness searches for and begins to apprehend the true meaning of existence and its upward goal. This experience is conveyed strikingly by one of the most beautiful *terzine* of the canto, when from within the narrow cleft in the rock,

> Poco parer potea lí del di fori;
>   ma, per quel poco, vedea io le stelle
>   di lor solere e piú chiare e maggiori.   88-90

Reflection is converted into contemplation, contemplation into serene sleep and prophetic dreaming, each following the other in a slow rhythm of natural, untroubled succession.

All three dreams in the *Purgatorio* spring from the pilgrim's state of mind which reflects a particular aspect of his moral state, the sinful disposition from which he has to free himself. At the same time each dream presages a further stage of spiritual progress with the revelation of higher realities by a process of augury and premonition in dream. Thus from the incursion by the serpent into "la picciola vallea" (*Purg.*viii.98) of the Kings and Princes representing "the involuntary aberrations of the unconscious",[13] springs the dream in *Purgatorio* ix in which the pilgrim feels that he is carried by an eagle into the sphere of fire, and which foreshadows the entry into the sacramental ground of active penance; later reflecting on sloth, "e 'l pensamento in sogno trasmutai" (*Purg.*xviii.145), "I changed my musing into dream"; by autosuggestion his mind is beguiled by the alluring power of the "femmina balba" (*Purg.*xix.7), the stuttering female, who is the incarnation of the falsehood to be purged in the ensuing terraces.

Now, with perfect symmetry, from lust, which the fire has changed to love, there follows the last dream as a complement to the previous ones, to foretell the state of incipient perfection the pilgrim is about to reach. On the very threshold of Eden Dante dreams of Leah and Rachel, the Old Testament sisters, daughters of Laban, traditional personifications of the active and contemplative lives. In the secret life of the dreamer's unconscious the light of the stars gradually and harmoniously dissolves into the pure radiance of dawn, shown here in the primeval beauty of the planet Venus as it seems to repeat the miracle of its first appearance at the time of the creation. Its fervent love is reflected in the beauty of a young woman who, in the graceful rhythm of the verse, glides along, picking flowers, a gesture that becomes music:

> Ne l'ora, credo, che de l'orïente
>   prima raggiò nel monte Citerea,
>   che di foco d'amor par sempre ardente,
> giovane e bella in sogno mi parea
>   donna vedere andar per una landa
>   cogliendo fiori; e cantando dicea:
> 'Sappia qualunque il mio nome dimanda
>   ch'i' mi son Lia, e vo movendo intorno
>   le belle mani a farmi una ghirlanda.
> Per piacermi a lo specchio, qui m'addorno;
>   ma mia suora Rachel mai non si smaga
>   dal suo miraglio, e siede tutto giorno.
> Ell' è d'i suoi belli occhi veder vaga
>   com' io de l'addornarmi con le mani;
>   lei lo vedere, e me l'ovrare appaga'.   94-108

The music runs all through the sequence, modulating Leah's movements and words and the static but intense look of Rachel, until the melodic rhythm comes to a perfect close in the last line.

In a few *terzine* the poet has encompassed a perfectly enchanting picture where music, colour, ethereal beauty combine harmoniously with a precise allegorical meaning. A reader of *poesia pura* like Attilio Momigliano is attracted by the formal elements of the passage. He notes that "Lia non dice che va 'cogliendo fiori', ma 'vo movendo intorno le belle mani a farmi una ghirlanda', sottolineando il ritmo delle mani e la loro bellezza; e tutto il resto della sua parlata vagheggia amorosamente la sua figura e quella della sorella: sicché tutto si move ancora in un'aura di canto e d'incanto, e il lettore amante della poesia non si sente frastornato dall'allegoria."[14] But it is possible to enjoy the poetry and appreciate at the same time the relevance of the symbol, without being distracted by it.[15] The reader, though fascinated by the captivating image, must heed the poet's primary intention in writing these lines. Poetic figure and symbol are totally blended. The symbolism needs no subtle interpretation. As symbolism it is plainly meant to illustrate how the wide perspective of fruitful action and contemplation, which are the two complementary aspects of the Christian life, now opens to the soul that has conquered itself. And the active and contemplative will recur more concretely in the figures of Matelda and Beatrice shortly afterwards. In the vision Leah is made to appear young and beautiful in contrast to the mature and rather plain woman described in Genesis (29.16 ff; 30.17 ff; 49.31), because the poet wishes to concentrate his and our attention on the inner qualities of her nature. The fertility of Jacob's Old Testament wife is here transformed into the industriousness of the hands preparing a garland for self-adornment. Leah is a work of love and her work is a work of love. She thus embodies the idealization of all forms of human activity, intellectual and practical, the moral value of every earthly endeavour inspired by virtue and sanctified by grace and her very complacency reflects the natural happiness of man.

But even in such an ideal state human happiness cannot be an end in itself. It must tend to a more specifically spiritual form of gratification which only contemplation of the transcendent can give. The one is actually the basis of the other. It is a question of distinction, not of opposition; perfection lies in the integration of the two lives. If Leah is to look at the mirror of her soul, Rachel has the image of her countenance in God's mirror, to Leah's hands correspond Rachel's eyes. It may be inappropriate, if not dangerous to apply modern concepts to a medieval text, but I think that in these two Dantean figures one could detect the notions, in Christian terms, of horizontality and verticality, of which the theologians of our time speak, and also the harmonization of the two may be said to find expression in Dante's poetic text. Of course in a total vision of human destiny the poet is aware that the contemplative life is superior to the active: Beatrice will take over from Matelda. But at this point of his moral and spiritual development the pilgrim is made aware of the intrinsic validity and sanctity of human life even in a supernatural perspective.

All this, however, has been intuited in the prophetic dream and its relevance will be clarified, mimetically and intellectually, in the last part of the canto.

> E già per li splendori antelucani,
>   che tanto a' pellegrin surgon piú grati,
>   quanto, tornando, albergan men lontani,
>   le tenebre fuggian da tutti lati,
>   e 'l sonno mio con esse; ond' io leva'mi,
>   veggendo i gran maestri già levati. 109-14

As every so often in the *Purgatorio* and particularly in this canto, the alteration in the colour of the sky mirrors the inner changes in the pilgrim's inner state. This time the triumph of light over darkness, reflecting the joy of the wayfarer's homecoming, marks the beginning of a new day, a special day. And Dante rises with a new sense of excitement, tempered somewhat by the austere look of Virgil and Statius. The phrase, "gran maestri già levati" (114), sums up all the wisdom dispensed by them during the journey and at the same time seems to underline their awareness of the momentous event

about to take place. That very day, announces Virgil, Dante
will taste the sweet fruit which will satisfy his hunger (115-17).
But in Virgil's arboreal metaphor the whole of mankind, in its
unending search for happiness, is associated with the pilgrim
who, in his own mind and flesh, has experienced how elusive
and unfulfilling are misdirected knowledge, glory, pleasure,
which are mere

> imagini di ben seguendo false,
> che nulla promession rendono intera, *Purg*.xxx.131-2

and for which Beatrice will once again reprimand him.

   Before they set out to climb Virgil had said to his disciple
that the mountain is hard to begin with, less toilsome later on:

> Ed elli a me: 'Questa montagna è tale,
>   che sempre al cominciar di sotto è grave;
>   e quant' om più va sú, e men fa male.
> Però, quand' ella ti parrà soave
>   tanto, che sú andar ti fia leggero
>   com' a seconda giú andar per nave,
> allor sarai al fin d'esto sentiero;
>   quivi di riposar l'affanno aspetta.'   *Purg*.iv.88-95

That moment has arrived as predicted. At Virgil's words Dante
dashes upwards, covering the last steps not so much with the
speed of a boat going downstream (*Purg*.iv.93) as with the
impetus of flight to reach the top:

> Tanto voler sopra voler mi venne
>   de l'esser sú, ch'ad ogne passo poi
>   al volo mi sentia crescer le penne.
> Come la scala tutta sotto noi
>   fu corsa . . .   121-5

   A whole series of stylistic devices is employed here by the
poet to convey the tension of mind and body. He uses

repetition in "voler . . . voler", alliteration in "voler" and "volo", "passo poi" and "penne", to indicate that his step takes wing. There is a strong caesura after "esser sú" and he makes use of a passive construction "fu corsa" with no mention of the agent and so renders very effectively the dashing motion. This intensive use of language will govern Virgil's last speech also, though there is a more calm staccato cadence in these *terzine*:

> e disse: 'Il temporal foco e l'etterno
> veduto hai, figlio; e se' venuto in parte
> dov' io per me piú oltre non discerno.
> Tratto t'ho qui con ingegno e con arte;
> lo tuo piacere omai prendi per duce;
> fuor se' de l'erte vie, fuor se' de l'arte.
> Vedi lo sol che 'n fronte ti riluce;
> vedi l'erbette, i fiori e li arbuscelli
> che qui la terra sol da sé produce.
> Mentre che vegnan lieti li occhi belli
> che, lagrimando, a te venir mi fenno,
> seder ti puoi e puoi andar tra elli.
> Non aspettar mio dir piú né mio cenno;
> libero, dritto e sano è tuo arbitrio,
> e fallo fora non fare a suo senno:
> per ch'io te sovra te corono e mitrio'.   127-42

The sustained tone of Virgil's final words, solemn and dignified, can hardly conceal his sadness at the end of a wonderful relationship between master and pupil. Here in the idyllic setting of a self-generating nature where the re-created myth of the Golden Age enhances the poignant feeling of happiness lost and refound Dante, whose nature and will have been restored to true freedom, is no longer in need of human wisdom and human science. Virgil has fulfilled his mission and, being no longer competent to guide him higher, is about to leave his disciple's side and to return "tra color che son sospesi" (*Inf*.ii.52), who "sanza speme" live "in disio" (*Inf*.iv.42). But

Virgil carries in his heart "li occhi lucenti lagrimando" (*Inf*.ii.116), the light of two eyes bright with tears that had moved him to go and help a nearly-lost soul.

The acquisition of virtue has been slow and painful, but at the end of the road Dante, *homo viator,* has achieved that moral integrity and spiritual wholeness which is inner justice as well as innocence, similar to the virtue the progenitors of the race possessed in this earthly paradise. Moreover, his freedom to move on or to stay amongst "l'erbette, i fiori e li arbuscelli" (134), recalling as they do the idyllic setting of Leah's loving labours, this freedom tells us that he can freely pursue the active or contemplative life with the confidence of his new, undivided love, with the joy of the pure in heart. The sun, God's light, shines on him and will set no more on his path.

In the concluding *terzina* of the canto Virgil proclaims Dante master and lord over himself. Having conquered the unwholesome inclinations of the senses and of the psyche, his will has become truly free and in his conduct he will now pursue only the right path. With the words "corono" and "mitrio", however, Virgil is conferring on Dante no temporal or spiritual authority, nor is he exempting him from civil and ecclesiastic jurisdiction as some commentators maintain. With this intensive formula Virgil consecrates Dante's achievement of a maturity of moral judgement and as it were seals the important role he as mentor has played in this achievement. As a declaration of a coming-of-age this has appeared suspect to some critics like Ulrich Leo. Viewing Virgil's discourse in the context of the sharp rebuke Dante will shortly receive from Beatrice followed by his repentance and the final purifying rite, Leo holds that the pilgrim in reality has attained no such moral integrity and sees in Virgil's investiture "una umanistica illusione", as though the poet's undeclared intention were to make the reader question the validity of the investiture in relation to that higher perfection to which the pilgrim aspires.[16] It must be answered that Virgil has never been under any humanistic illusion. Throughout the journey he has been aware of reason's inability both to grasp the mysteries of the supernatural and to sense the mysterious ways grace works within man. Besides, the pilgrim's progress has been made possible mainly by the effective presence of sacramental signs, mainly but not exclusively. For human philosophy and human science, natural morality and natural reason have made a significant contribution to his enlightenment. Like nature these values have a beauty of their own since ultimately they also derive from God and even though they are relative and often inadequate, as Virgil himself frequently and tragically feels and recognizes, they are not negated but can be validated by Christian Revelation. Not "umanistica illusione" then, but Christian humanism or, if one prefers, Dante's Christian humanism. This is an ethical revaluation of the luminous legacy from the ancient world, a legacy which Christianity absorbed in so far as that world had been able to elaborate and express what was true, right and noble. From the initial cantos of the *Inferno* to this terminal phase of the *Purgatorio* Virgil is the unconscious prophet of Christianity and creator of an *opus poeticum* which to Dante was not only a model of *bello stile* but also and above all a religious vision of human history. He is therefore the voice of the ancient world and links its values with those of a superior world.

With sunset and twilight, with its deep night and radiant dawn where the visible cosmos adumbrates the invisible, with the dramatic passage through the fire inspired by Beatrice, with the song of the angels at each end of this last manifestation of human weakness and good will, with the dream of Leah opening up the wide perspective of fruitful action and mystical contemplation, *Purgatorio* xxvii epitomizes the complex theme of the second *cantica* and seals it with the affirmation that moral responsibility is the foundation of Christian freedom.

Notes

[1]Quoted and translated in R. Hollander, *Allegory in Dante's "Commedia"* (Princeton, 1969), p. 96.

[2]Each of the beatitudes is sung by the angel of every terrace while the letter P, the mark of each vice, is erased from the pilgrim's forehead and thus points to the virtues corrective of the seven deadly sins.

[3]Compare to this the passage:

> Io stava come 'l frate che confessa
> lo perfido assessin, che, poi ch'è fitto,
> richiama lui per che la morte cessa.   *Inf*.xix.49-51

[4]J. Sinclair for example, gives "I stretched up my clasped hands" as his version and avoids the difficulty by leaving out "mi"; J. Ciardi understands "in su" as meaning "up to the waist" and calls the gesture "oddly Dantean". I would suggest the following interpretation: "Bending over my clasped hands I stretched myself to test the flame, recoiling from it".

[5]N. Sapegno ed., *Purgatorio* (Florence, 1956), p. 301.

[6]In the translation by A. Colquhoun: A. Manzoni, *The Betrothed* (London, 1952), p. 3.

[7]See the commentary by M. Pazzaglia in *Nuove letture dantesche* (Florence, 1966—), V (1972), pp. 112-15.

[8]From the commentary by U. Leo in *Letture dantesche,* ed. G. Getto (Florence, 1963), p. 1219.

[9]See T. S. Eliot's definition of this term given above in note 3 to the reading by C. S. Lonergan of *Inferno* xxxiii.

[10]M. Pazzaglia, p. 116, see note 7.

[11]M. Pazzaglia, p. 120, see note 7.

[12]R. Montano, *Storia della poesia di Dante* (Naples, 1963), p. 216.

[13]D. L. Sayers, *The Divine Comedy*, II, *Purgatory* (London, 1955), p. 130.

[14]A. Momigliano ed., *Purgatorio* (Florence, 1947), p. 472.

[15]P. Calì, *Allegory and Vision in Dante and Langland* (Cork, 1971), pp. 85-6.
[16]U. Leo, pp. 1220-1. See also on this important point the commentary by A. Frattini in *Lectura Dantis Scaligera: Purgatorio* (Florence, 1967), pp. 995-1031.

Purgatorio XXVIII

Peter Armour

In this canto, one of the most celebrated and beautiful in the *Commedia*, Dante describes the earthly paradise, the garden of delights on the summit of the mountain of Purgatory. After the long climb up the mountain, Dante has been healed of the seven wounds, and, with the weight of his body now attenuated, he has been weaned from earthly attachments. In the journey through the terraces his love has been purified, directed away from bad objects, from negligence in the service of God and from excessive love of secondary goods and made coextensive with that innate natural love which all men have for God, Supreme Good, who alone can give that total happiness which each soul experienced at the moment of creation and to which it aspires ever afterwards. In this process of bringing his elective love together with his natural love into focus on the same object, supreme good, his will has been healed and made straight and Virgil has bestowed upon him the crown and the mitre, the freedom of perfect autonomy of the will in both the temporal and the spiritual spheres. Purged by the fire from the final attachment, excessive sensual love, he still, however, has one ordeal through which he must pass: his painful confession to Beatrice that after her death he strayed from her and gave his love to others, to vanities, to false images of good.

Between his acquisition of true liberty and his final confession to Beatrice, Dante is left free to explore the beautiful Garden of Eden where man once enjoyed perfect temporal happiness but from which he was expelled. For a little over six hours man lived in this paradise, then, because of the tree, it became a paradise lost, a memory which lived on in the Old Testament, perhaps also even in the poetry of pagans, but which could never be regained by mankind living in exile in the corrupt northern hemisphere. Some five thousand years after the Fall a new Adam who was also God was crucified to a tree on a hill on the opposite side of the earth at the centre of the northern hemisphere and so to mankind was given again the possibility of revisiting the lost paradise in the south, on the high mountain barred to pagans but open to saved Christians in their journey after death from corrupt earth to the heavenly paradise. Here, in the earthly paradise, at the highest point on earth, diametrically opposite Jerusalem, Dante undergoes the final stages of his purification before leaving the earth altogether and ascending to the eternal paradise, the "garden of the eternal gardener" (*Par*.xxvi.64-5), the eternal spring of spiritual happiness with its river of light and the rose of the blessed flowering under the rays of the true sun, God.

The earthly paradise prefigures the heavenly paradise. It was given to man as his home on earth, a place of ineffable delights and happiness, a place of peace, free from storms, but not the ultimate reality, only an anticipation, a pledge of true eternal peace in the heavenly paradise. Now, however, this shaded forest, man's original home on earth, is empty because of the sin of Eve (*Purg*.xxxii.31-2). Man has been banished to the corrupt part of earth where is the dark wood from which Dante has escaped. The garden where, but for sin, man would have lived in happiness can now be regained only by the souls of the dead who are saved, but by a special dispensation one living man, Dante, now purified from the effects of sin, may visit and explore and describe it in his poem for the benefit of mankind still living amid sin and corruption on the other side of the earth.

In the *Monarchia* Dante treats the earthly paradise as a symbol of the ideal of earthly happiness:

> God's ineffable Providence has given man two goals to strive for: namely, happiness in this life, which consists in the active use of one's own powers and is symbolized by the Earthly Paradise; and the happiness of eternal life which consists in the enjoyment of the sight of God to which one's own powers cannot attain unless assisted by divine light, and this is to be understood as the Heavenly Paradise. (*Mon*.III.xv.7)

It is clear, however, that the earthly paradise which Dante explores in *Purgatorio* xxviii is not to be taken as a mere symbol of temporal felicity but as a real place with a precise geographical location, a place in which man had once really enjoyed the happiness of this life but which for fallen man can now only be a symbol of a desired ideal of earthly happiness attainable in reality only by the souls of the saved on their way to the ultimate ideal and reality of heavenly happiness. So the garden is a real place which simultaneously evokes nostalgia for a lost ideal of earthly happiness and prefigures the final ideal of eternal happiness in heaven.

The Book of Genesis had described the delightful paradise or garden planted by God to be the home of man:

> The Lord God had planted the paradise of pleasure from the beginning, and in it he placed man whom he had formed. And the Lord God produced from the earth all kinds of trees, beautiful to behold and sweet to eat: also the tree of life in the middle of the paradise, and the tree of the

knowledge of good and evil. And a river came forth from
the place of pleasure to irrigate the paradise, and later it is
divided into four springs. The name of one is Phison . . .
And the name of the second river is Gehon . . . And the
name of the third river is Tigris, and the fourth river is the
Euphrates. So the Lord God took man and placed him in
the paradise of pleasure that he might work and guard over
it. (Genesis, 2, 8-15)

In this garden on earth man was to work, to guard over it, to
lead an active life, developing his personal powers within a
realm of perfect temporal happiness. But man fell and was
expelled to northern lands to till a cursed earth, to toil among
thorns and thistles, to earn his bread by the sweat of his brow,
and to die, returning to the earth from which he came (Genesis,
3, 17-19).

From this biblical account of the paradise which man had
lost there arose many legends about its location and its
beauties. According to a variation in the Latin Bible it was
sometimes placed in the east, cut off from the inhabited earth,
on a mountain which reached up to the sphere of the moon.
Christian and Mohammedan mythology equipped it with
magical trees and plants and with guardians; for Christians,
Enoch or Elijah, for Mohammedans, seductive houris. Dante
cuts away all these superstitious and even unedifying
accretions. His earthly paradise is the original garden planted
by God from the beginning, unspoilt nature whose existence
still depends directly on the creative power of God and the
heavenly spheres, a primeval living forest of eternal spring but,
except for one beautiful lady, empty.[1]

Dante's presentation of the garden as a forest derives from
such sources as St. Augustine's description of it as "darkened
by fruitful groves",[2] but no doubt Dante was also thinking of
the antithesis with the wild, cruel forest in which, on the other
side of the world, he had lost his way. Also in his mind are the
forests of classical poets, groves inhabited by nymphs of light

and nymphs of the shadows (*Purg.*xxix.4-6), and the classical myth of the Golden Age of man, when the human race was innocent, living in a world of spring and natural love, among rivers of milk and nectar. Indeed, the whole canto, describing the biblical Garden of Eden, is woven through with classical reminiscences which culminate in the beautiful lady's statement that maybe the classical poets too had their intuition of this Christian truth of man's original innocence and subsequent fall. Into the biblical and Christian waters over which the boat of Dante's poetic genius sails there flows and mingles that other stream of his inspiration, the classics, bringing this canto to a close with the intimate, unspoken interaction of three poets at their recognition of this possible confluence of truth in all poetry, both Christian and pagan.

It is in the earthly paradise too that Dante meets a new guide, the "bella donna", who takes over from Virgil and Statius and looks after Dante until Beatrice arrives to guide him to the heavenly paradise. When Dante sees her, across the stream, picking flowers and singing, she is the marvellous fulfilment of his prophetic dream of Leah, who was using her hands to weave a garland for herself, and who represents the active life using her own powers in this life to adorn herself with virtue and fame and so proceed after death to salvation and true immortality in the eternal contemplative joys of Heaven.[3] In the earthly paradise, the lost place of innocence, a real lady now appears to Dante amid the vernal beauties of unspoilt nature; she is full of love as she picks her flowers and sings her song with its unheard words; she turns like a lady dancing, modest as a virgin;her eyes shine with love. In this presentation of the young and beautiful woman all alone in a pastoral setting of spring and flowers, Dante draws on the whole medieval tradition of describing the beauty of woman, with reminiscences of the *pastourelle* and of the poetry of his own younger days. So, with this lady, the three sources of Dante's poetry come together: the biblical, for she fulfils the dream of Leah; the classical, for she immediately reminds Dante of

Proserpina; and the *dolce stil novo*, in the pastoral setting, in her singing, her slow pirouette, and her modesty, in the light of her eyes and the joy of her smile.

This beautiful lady is "soletta", all alone, the only inhabitant of the Garden of Eden since man was cast out because of the sin of Eve. She belongs to the world of the "sweet apple", the goal of all man's various endeavours to gain happiness on earth (*Purg.*xxvii.115-7). She is part of what Adam and Eve lost when they sinned. As the diminutive "soletta", the comparison to Proserpina, and the references to her small steps (*Purg.*xxviii.52-4 and xxix.9) indicate, she is still young, eternally young, in this garden of perpetual spring.

But who is she? Is she a purely symbolic figure to be connected, on the one hand, with Leah, symbol of the active life, and, on the other hand, with the allegorical procession of *Purgatorio* xxix? Or is she, like Virgil, Cato, Statius, and Beatrice, the soul of a real person with a divinely appointed function in the afterlife and in the poem? Moreover, if she is purely a symbol, why after a gap of five cantos is Dante informed that her name is Matelda? And if she is the shade of a real Matelda, which Matelda is she? The Countess of Tuscany, a St. Matilda, or a lady whom Dante knew? Every student of Dante knows that the problem of the identity of Matelda is one of the most perplexing in the whole poem.[4] To solve it, if it ever can be satisfactorily solved, would require a review of about twenty theories and would raise complex questions concerning the whole history of Dante's poetry and the fundamental symbolic structure of the entire *Commedia*. This is obviously beyond the scope of this reading. Nevertheless, within the context of this one canto, it is possible to define the essential function and meaning of this young and beautiful lady in a way which makes her, paradoxically, a symbol with a special reality, for to Dante she is undoubtedly very real. In this investigation we must pass over the meaning of her name, Matelda, and leave aside her later duties in the earthly paradise, which are to lead Dante to the procession, take him through the waters of the Lethe, present him to the four nymphs who represent the cardinal virtues, and give him to drink of the waters of the Eunoè.

When Dante first sees this lady, he does not seem to recognise her, and so she cannot be at this moment a girl whom he really knew. Nor does she at this stage evoke in the mind of the reader any association with any saint or other known historical person. The sight of her all alone in the garden astonishes Dante. The person who looks after the paradise and joyfully plucks its flowers is not the ancient Enoch, nor can she be Eve who was cast out thousands of years before and is now in Heaven. This lady still resides in the garden, eternally young and all alone. Indeed she is a mysterious and astonishing apparition, for the reader as for Dante. Who is she and what can she represent? Critics have seen her as a symbol of original innocence, or natural justice, or the happiness of this life, or even as the object of some sort of sensual love which possesses Dante, even though now he is purified.[5] These theories, however, miss the fact that the lady herself defines her own function in this very canto: she has come specifically to answer all Dante's questions in the intervening period before Beatrice comes (83-4); twice she talks of clearing his mind of mist, that is, of imparting knowledge to him (lines 81 and 90); in fact, she is throughout this episode his instructress, teaching him the cause of the breeze, the growth of the plants, and the source and function of the two rivers, and generously adding a corollary of particular interest to her audience of three poets. At the same time she lives in the garden from which Adam and Eve were cast out, and she sings joyfully in praise of the Creator and his creation.

All these things — the primeval setting in Eden, her function as teacher, and her joy in creation — might well remind the reader of that lady in the Old Testament who proclaims:

I came forth from the mouth of the Most High, the firstborn before all creation . . . From the beginning and before the ages I was created, and up to the future age I shall not cease, and I ministered before him in a holy dwelling-place. And so I am established in Sion, and I rested likewise in a sanctified city . . . I am exalted like a cedar in Lebanon and like a cypress on Mount Sion . . . as a fair olive-tree in the fields . . . Like a vine I have brought forth sweet-scented fruit, and my flowers are the fruits of honour and of virtue . . . Cross over to me all you who desire me . . . [The Lord] fills wisdom as the Phison, and as the Tigris in the days of the new fruits; he fills understanding as the Euphrates . . . attending as the Gehon in the day of the wine-harvest . . . I, wisdom, poured forth the rivers. I, like a branch of a river of mighty water, like a bed of a river, like a channel of water, I came from the paradise. I said: I will water my garden of plants, and I will inebriate the fruit of my field. (Ecclesiasticus 24, 5-42)

The Lord possessed me in the beginning of his ways, before anything was made from the beginning. From eternity I was established, and from times of old before the earth existed. The depths did not exist, and I had been conceived; the fountains of waters had not yet sprung forth; the mountains with their heavy bulk did not exist; I was born before the hills. He had not yet made the earth or the rivers or the pivots of the world. When he prepared the heavens, I was there; when with his sure law and his compass he surrounded the depths, when he established the heavens above and balanced the fountains of the waters, when he surrounded the sea with its boundary and laid down his law upon the waters that they should not overstep their limits, when he attached the foundations of the world, I was with him, fashioning all things, and I was delighted [*delectabar*] every day, playing before him all the time, playing in the world, and my delight was to be with the children of men. (Proverbs 8, 22-31)

This biblical lady, the firstborn of creation, who tends the flowers and fruits of paradise, who rejoices in creation, and who lived with mankind, is Wisdom.[6] She is the teacher of virtues and the bestower of immortality (Wisdom 8, 7; Proverbs 8, 14; Ecclesiasticus 15, 5-6); she appears joyfully to those who seek her (Wisdom 6, 17); she makes them love her form and want to take her as a bride (Wisdom 8, 2); like a mother or a virgin bride she takes the just man, feeds him on the bread of life and understanding, and gives him to drink of the water of saving wisdom (Ecclesiasticus 15, 2-3). She looked over Adam when he was first created and helped him even after his sin, but she was abandoned by Cain when he killed his brother (Wisdom 10, 1-3). Solomon loved her and she was given to him to teach him:

> [The Lord] gave me true knowledge of everything which exists, that I might know the disposition of the world, and the powers of the elements, the beginning and the end and the middle of the ages, the changes of their variations, and the alterations of the seasons, the courses of the year, and the dispositions of the stars, the nature of animals and the passion of beasts, the power of the winds and the thoughts of men, the differences of plants and the powers [*virtutes*] of roots, and I learnt all things hidden and unforeseen, for wisdom, the maker of all things, taught me . . . For she is a vapour of the power of God and a pure emanation of the brightness of the almighty God . . . For she is the brightness of eternal light and a spotless mirror of the majesty of God and an image of his goodness. (Wisdom 7, 17-21, and 25-6)[7]

Here are all the elements required for understanding the beautiful lady of *Purgatorio* xxviii, eternally young, guardian of the paradise, rejoicing in God's works, and lost by man through sin; she is the source of the virtues of the active life, so fulfilling the dream of Leah; she is a mirror and an image of God's goodness, and her eyes reflect the light of his love. She

teaches her lover, Dante, the powers of the elements, the
heavens, the winds, the plants, and the "virtues" of roots, and
then, lest we should think her knowledge purely metereological
and botanical and be tempted to consider her purely a symbol
of *Philosophia naturalis*, this beautiful and all-knowing lady
adds a special postscript on classical poetry.

So Dante accepts the biblical style of presenting Wisdom as
a real lady, just as, in earlier years, he had made the "Donna
gentile" of the *Vita Nuova* a screen for his new love of another
lady, Lady Philosophy, who also was the daughter of God,
queen of all, most noble and most beautiful: "figlia di Dio,
regina di tutto, nobilissima e bellissima Filosofia" (*Conv.*
II.xii.9) and represented the habitual love of Wisdom
created before the ages. But this lady is not the "Donna gentile"
nor Lady Philosophy, for the latter was still in part pagan, and
both of these ladies made Dante unfaithful to Beatrice. This
lady is the Wisdom who takes over from pagan Virgil and from
Statius and teaches Dante the special secrets of the Garden of
Eden, who attends upon him while he confesses that he strayed
from Beatrice, and who then immerses him in the Lethe, giving
him, at last, oblivion from that infidelity. These biblical texts
concerning primeval Wisdom were, moreover, commonly used
in the liturgy to refer to Mary, the new Eve who healed the sin
of Adam, so that this virgin who tends the lost paradise belongs
to both eras, the Old Testament and the New, being associated
with Eve and Leah, with the Madonna and Beatrice. She also
includes knowledge of classical poetry and is compared by
Dante to Proserpina and to Venus. For all these reasons she is
presented with a wealth of biblical, classical, and stilnovistic
detail, and yet she remains always herself, not Eve, not Mary,
not Lady Philosophy, but the beautiful lady who tends the
paradise. In the figure of this lady, in her wisdom and in her
love of creation and in Dante's love of her, he has brought to its
ultimate stage his picture of all those ladies in his life who were
not Beatrice: the screen-ladies and Beatrice's companions in
the *Vita Nuova*, the "Donna gentile", and Lady Philosophy;

and now his love for her is absolutely pure (for he is in the garden of innocence) and it will lead him to Beatrice. She presents herself to his imagination in all the youth and freshness of his own earlier poetry, but now she is met in the rich moral and poetic context of Eden, of a paradise on earth, once lost by Eve and now regained by Dante. So she is not merely a symbol but the reality of the primeval Wisdom hymned by Solomon, the perfected and purified lady of Wisdom loved by Dante in younger days, and one of the realities of his journey through the afterlife, a real person appointed by God to instruct and to perform the final rites of purification in the earthly paradise. This, fundamentally, is why Dante later gives her a real name: Matelda.

Purgatorio xxviii is essentially a description of an exploration and an acquisition of knowledge. Dante has escaped from a "selva selvaggia e aspra e forte" (*Inf.*i.5) and has arrived here at its opposite, a "divina foresta spessa e viva" (2). By travelling through Hell and Purgatory he has learnt how man can escape from sin and arrive once more at the place where mankind was once, though but briefly, sinless. Virgil has promised him the sweet apple which will appease his hunger, has told him that until Beatrice comes he may either sit down or wander through the garden, and has given him complete freedom to follow his own purified will. Characteristically, it is not for Dante to sit down and enjoy it idly, but he is filled with the desire to explore the paradise, to discover its secrets, and so to become able to describe its beauties to his readers as an enticement to them to make the same journey as he from earth to God.

The opening lines of this canto of exploration establish the psychological state of the explorer. Already Virgil's words have filled his enquiring mind and purified will with an intense desire to use the time available to acquire vital knowledge of man's earthly paradise, to find out all he can about the thick and living forest, dark and mysterious in the morning sun:

Vago già di cercar dentro e dintorno
la divina foresta spessa e viva,
ch'a li occhi temperava il novo giorno,
sanza piú aspettar, lasciai la riva.   1-4

Having reached the place of natural innocence and peace
unknown to man in the northern hemisphere, he immediately
sets off to explore it,

prendendo la campagna lento lento
su per lo suol che d'ogne parte auliva.   5-6

The slow, measured steps of the explorer establish the
tranquillity of will, the calm certainty of the man who is slowly
acquiring experience of this changeless, peaceful world. His
first experiences are of unhurried sensual enjoyment, for the
paradisus voluptatis is, first and foremost, a world which
delights the senses. The first sense to be so affected is his sense
of smell, filled with the all-pervading fragrance of the garden:
"lo suol che d'ogne parte auliva" (6). Then his sense of touch is
involved, as the rare word "auliva", expressing the primeval
and eternal nature of the fragrance, is linked by its vowel-
sound and gives way to a description of the gentle, unchanging
"aura" upon which the scent is borne:

Un'aura dolce, sanza mutamento
avere in sé, mi feria per la fronte
non di piú colpo che soave vento;
per cui le fronde, tremolando, pronte
tutte quante piegavano a la parte
u' la prim' ombra gitta il santo monte.   7-12

This soft and steady breeze which lightly caresses Dante's brow
is the west wind, bringer of spring, which makes all the leaves
quiver and bend away from where the sun sets and towards the

east where the sun is now rising. The steady sound of the leaves
is anticipated in the quiet assonance of "le fronde, tremolando,
pronte tutte quante"(10), but what is stressed here is above all
the harmony of nature, as the changeless breeze bends all of the
leaves in the same direction towards the rising sun, and yet so
gently that it does not interfere with the little birds which
joyfully sing to the morning as it comes to the forest. There is
complete harmony of the breeze, the leaves, the little birds, all
directed towards the rising sun:

> non però dal loro esser dritto sparte
>   tanto, che li augelletti per le cime
>   lasciasser d'operare ogne lor arte;
> ma con piena letizia l'ore prime,
>   cantando, ricevieno intra le foglie,
>   che tenevan bordone a le sue rime,
> tal qual di ramo in ramo si raccoglie
>   per la pineta in su 'l lito di Chiassi,
>   quand' Ëolo scilocco fuor discioglie.   13-21

The birds' chorus, accompanied by the rustling of the leaves,
is the first gratification of the sense of hearing. Together they
make music, the music of nature, in which the birds' joyful song
to the morning is accompanied by the steady *organum* of the
wind in the leaves. The experience, as so often with music in
Dante, draws his imagination into a simile taken from his own
experience, in this case the pinewoods near Ravenna, and the
description is enriched by onomatopoeia and elevated by a
classical allusion. So the experience is presented as real and
natural but at the same time ancient and changeless, the sound
of leaves moved by an eternal sirocco, the steadiest of winds.

    After this account of the harmony of nature in the garden of
delights, the narrative moves to a further level of exploration.
Dante's slow steps have taken him into the shaded depths of the
ancient forest, where he is suddenly brought to a halt by a
stream:

Già m'avean trasportato i lenti passi
   dentro a la selva antica tanto, ch'io
   non potea rivedere ond' io mi 'ntrassi;
ed ecco piú andar mi tolse un rio,
   che 'nver' sinistra con sue picciole onde
   piegava l'erba che 'n sua ripa uscío.
Tutte l'acque che son di qua piú monde,
   parrieno avere in sé mistura alcuna
   verso di quella, che nulla nasconde,
avvegna che si mova bruna bruna
   sotto l'ombra perpetüa, che mai
   raggiar non lascia sole ivi né luna.   22-33

The stream is described first of all in its reality, as a natural
feature of the garden. It flows to the left, its gentle ripples
bending the grass at its edge; its waters are clearer than the
clearest waters known in man's part of the world; its ceaseless,
steady flow is conveyed by the repetition of the word "bruna".
But already there is a foretaste of the river's function, for,
unlike the breeze, the leaves, and the birds, the stream is to play
an important part in the final purification of Dante. It is, as we
are soon to find out, the Lethe, the classical river of oblivion,
and so Dante matches its absolute, all-revealing purity with its
darkness under the perpetual shade, impenetrable to light of
sun or moon. In a short time Dante will be told of the two rivers
which take the place of the four rivers of Eden described in the
Bible; later, he will be immersed in these waters and will gain
oblivion from his infidelity to Beatrice; later still, his sense of
taste will be delighted by the sweet waters of the companion-
river, the Eunoè, which flows from the same source. For the
moment, however, this dark, limpid river is a barrier which
stops him in his tracks and prevents him exploring the garden
any further, except with his eyes.

Coi piè ristetti e con li occhi passai
   di là dal fiumicello, per mirare
   la gran varïazion d'i freschi mai.   34-6

Looking across the river, Dante first admires the great variety
of fresh flowers and blossoms "la gran varïazion d'i freschi
mai" (36). In its unusual metre this is one of the most bounding
and joyful of Dante's lines, and in its choice of words it
expresses not only the freshness and the great variety of species
and colour but also the theme of spring, for the word "mai"
refers to the flowers and blossomed branches put at doors and
windows on May Day.[8]

> E là m'apparve, sí com' elli appare
>   subitamente cosa che disvia
>   per maraviglia tutto altro pensare,
> una donna soletta che si gia
>   e cantando e scegliendo fior da fiore
>   ond' era pinta tutta la sua via.   37-42

In this scene of spring and flowers there appears a figure whose
presence in the garden both astonishes Dante and attracts his
total attention. This lady, young and all alone, "soletta",
singing and carefully choosing and picking the coloured
flowers, is the fulfilment of his dream of Leah who picked
flowers in order to make herself more beautiful in Heaven. This
lady attracts Dante with her beauty and the expression of love
on her face, which he knows must reflect the love in her heart.
He also realises that this love is the warming light which comes
from above and that it is love from Heaven.

> 'Deh, bella donna, che a' raggi d'amore
>   ti scaldi, s'i' vo' credere a' sembianti
>   che soglion esser testimon del core,
> vegnati in voglia di trarreti avanti',
>   diss'io a lei, 'verso questa rivera,
>   tanto ch'io possa intender che tu canti.'   43-8

Dante, barred by the river, wishes above all to hear her song,
the words which express her fullness of heavenly love. This love

which he recognises in her is certainly not love for him, for this beautiful lady who so absorbs his eyes and mind is still alone, wrapped in her own singing and in her task of picking flowers, distant from Dante, unaware of him. This sense of distance in space and through ages of time is immediately reinforced when, to his impassioned appeal for knowledge of her song, Dante adds:

> 'Tu mi fai rimembrar dove e qual era
> Proserpina nel tempo che perdette
> la madre lei, ed ella primavera.'   49-51

With this, the first of three references to classical mythology in the episode of the "bella donna", Dante recalls the Ovidian myth of Proserpina abducted while she was picking flowers in the vale of Henna in Sicily and taken to be the bride of Pluto in the underworld.[9] This sudden intrusion of a classical allusion into a biblical context may surprise, but it is, as we have seen, part of the stylistic texture of the whole canto and an anticipation of the lady's closing words on the dreams of classical poets. The allusion itself is complex. The early commentators see the reference to the myth of Proserpina and her mother, Ceres, as an allegory of the earth and spring,[10] and it is true that the themes of spring, innocence, virginity, and a beautiful woman belonging to the dawn of history are all appropriate to the portrayal of a beautiful woman picking flowers in a garden of eternal spring. Yet Dante says something more. He concentrates on Proserpina at the very moment of her abduction and her farewell to her mother. The word "perdette" introduces the double loss, Ceres's loss of her daughter and the daughter's loss of spring, which fills line 51, as it contrasts "la madre" and "primavera" around the pivot of the two pronouns "lei" and "ella", with condensed pathos of which Dante was a master:

> 'nel tempo che perdette
> la madre lei, ed ella primavera.'   50-1

Moreover, the syntax is ambiguous. The first part of the sentence makes one read: at the time when she lost her mother. The second part then forces an interchange of the previous subject and object, but as the reader is made to reread the sentence the possibility arises that "ella" could refer to the mother. Again one corrects to the only satisfactory sense, in which both "lei" and "ella" refer to Proserpina, one as the object, the other as the subject of the same verb "perdette" but the syntactical ambiguity has already raised the image not just of a double but of a quadruple loss: a daughter has lost a mother and a mother a daughter; the daughter has lost her spring, her flowers,[11] her virginity, and the mother, too, in losing her daughter, has lost spring. In the allegory earth loses spring, and spring leaves the earth; the cycle of the seasons has begun.

Why should Dante at this point stress the idea of the loss of spring? Surely as part of the theme of the paradise lost. The beautiful lady reminds Dante of a primeval figure of spring just at the moment before it was lost. Through eating the pomegranate Proserpina was taken from spring, although for six months each year she was to be allowed to return; through eating the apple Eve lost the eternal spring of the earthly paradise permanently. Dante could not use the image of Eve here because the whole point is that Eve was expelled from the garden whilst Matelda is still there. Instead, through the reference to Proserpina at the moment of her abduction and loss, he gives to Matelda the qualities of Eve before the Fall, "femmina, sola e pur testé formata" (*Purg*.xxix.26), newly created in all her fresh innocence and beauty. Matelda, however, still lives in the garden, a virgin Proserpina fixed forever in her spring and innocence; the other equivalent to Proserpina, Eve, ancient mother of mankind, lost her spring and was sent to a world of change, with autumn and winter, ageing and death. Into the line describing Proserpina's loss and the loss of Proserpina, Dante has compressed the whole tragedy of Eve's fall and of man's loss of his earthly paradise. In revisiting the paradise and in meeting Matelda, Dante is regaining what Eve, like Proserpina, enjoyed for so very short a time.

The classical reference is immediately succeeded by two realistic similes. The first, the simile of the lady in a slow dance, describes a perceived action. Matelda's unhurried turn matches the timeless harmony of the garden; her small, precise steps imply youth and modesty; the bright flowers beneath her feet set off her own beauty and so earn the endearing diminutive "fioretti",[12] like the "erbette" (*Purg.*xxvii.134), the "augelletti", the "fiumicello" of the garden and the adjective "soletta" applied to the lady herself. The second simile, of the virgin with lowered eyes, is psychological, continuing the themes of youth and innocence within the context of the inner personality, self-contained, virtuous, and pure. The whole passage is both realistic and reminiscent of the *dolce stil novo* in its delicate treatment of femininity in a setting of natural beauty complemented by inner virtue.

Graciously the lady answers Dante's request and allows him to hear the words of her song. We are never told exactly what her song is, but, as she later explains, it is clearly connected with the psalm *Delectasti* and her joy in the beauties of God's creation. So, after the sweet natural music of the birds and rustling leaves, there comes to Dante a further, but undescribed, musical experience, a human song of praise to God for his wonderful creation.

> Come si volge, con le piante strette
>   a terra e intra sé, donna che balli,
>   e piede innanzi piede a pena mette,
> volsesi in su i vermigli e in su i gialli
>   fioretti verso me, non altrimenti
>   che vergine che li occhi onesti avvalli;
> e fece i prieghi miei esser contenti,
>   sí appressando sé, che 'l dolce suono
>   veniva a me co' suoi intendimenti.   52-60

When she arrives at the very edge of the stream, the lady raises her eyes, and the effect on Dante is overwhelming. His vision of this sudden burst of the light of love is described by means of the second classical allusion to Venus when, accidentally pierced by Cupid's arrow, she shone with love for Adonis. Here the classical comparison is part of Dante's regular technique in describing the supernatural marvels of the afterlife: the light of love in Matelda's eyes exceeds what Dante imagines must have been that of Venus, the goddess of love herself, at the moment when her most extraordinary and intense love was born. The greatest love conceivable in human terms is surpassed by the divine love which shines in Matelda's eyes. The supernatural world exceeds any natural or even mythological equivalent, and in this respect it seems that the phrase "fuor di tutto suo costume" should be taken to refer, not to Cupid's carelessness with his arrows, but to the unusual intensity of Venus's love at that moment. We are certainly not intended to think here of sensual passion, of the "folle amore" of pagan deities (*Par.*viii.2), but of the way in which divine love is beyond any love known at any time on earth.

> Tosto che fu là dove l'erbe sono
>   bagnate già da l'onde del bel fiume,
>   di levar li occhi suoi mi fece dono.
> Non credo che splendesse tanto lume
>   sotto le ciglia a Venere, trafitta
>   dal figlio fuor di tutto suo costume.   61-6

Then, as with the ladies celebrated by Dante and by other poets of the *dolce stil novo*, the sight of her love-bearing eyes is followed by the sight of her smile, expressing her inner spiritual joy. The presentation of Matelda's appearance ends with a *terzina* which fixes her in our minds with her shining eyes, her smile, and the motion of her hands as, like the Leah of the dream, she plaits her garland with the beautiful multicoloured flowers of the marvellous garden:

> Ella ridea da l'altra riva dritta,
> trattando piú color con le sue mani,
> che l'alta terra sanza seme gitta.   67-9

With this vision, the inspiration of so many later poets, fixed before our eyes, there is a dramatic change. Our minds are suddenly focused on Dante's inner state, as his attention turns to the river, the river as an obstacle, small but impassable, between him and this beautiful lady. The rapt concentration, culminating in the full sight of Matelda's eyes and smile, is replaced by a fierce resentment, indeed a hatred, of the barrier which separates him from her:

> Tre passi ci facea il fiume lontani;
> ma Elesponto, là 've passò Serse,
> ancora freno a tutti orgogli umani,
> piú odio da Leandro non sofferse
> per mareggiare intra Sesto e Abido,
> che quel da me perch' allor non s'aperse.   70-5

Using a classical allusion to the love of Leander for Hero across the Hellespont, Dante indicates his intense desire to join this beautiful lady across the water. His desire for her cannot be sensual, for he has only just been purified from excessive sensual love, and any return to it would be a further betrayal of Beatrice and in the garden of innocence too. But, as we have seen, it could well be that love for someone other than Beatrice, a love, that is, which began with the "Donna gentile" and then became a love for Lady Philosophy, and which is now presented in its final purified stage, the natural and innocent desire for truth and wisdom which is now not a betrayal of Beatrice but a necessary stage in returning to her. Once again the great but exclusively earthly love of Leander for Hero in mythological times must be transferred to the story of a journey through the afterlife, a journey to Matelda first, then to Beatrice and finally to God.

Moreover, the essential function of this classical comparison is to convey, not so much Dante's love for Matelda as his bitterness against the barrier between them, the river which excludes him from enjoying the full delights of the garden and renders fruitless his desire to join this lady and participate in her love and happiness. His animosity against this barrier is condensed into a rich and complex image which consists of three elements: Dante hates the little river more than Leander hated the Hellespont separating him from Hero; the Hellespont is itself a constant warning to man to restrain his pride, for Xerxes, who proudly crossed it with his vast army, was to recross it, as Benvenuto says, "like a hare or timid mouse, after humiliating defeat on land and sea, in a small boat without even a servant"; and finally, Dante wants the river to part, as the Red Sea did for Moses, so that he may cross. In other words, Dante is Leander at the moment when he is acutely aware of his separation, not the Leander who did in fact swim across the Hellespont and was drowned, for his love was earthly; Dante does not think of swimming but of the waters parting, an impossible miracle, emphasizing again the theme of a separation which is, for the time being, absolute. In between, the reference to Xerxes and to the Hellespont as a moral warning against pride is also an image of a barrier, of limits set by God which proud man must not presume to cross. Ulysses had crossed forbidden waters, and his punishment in Hell had reminded Dante to keep a bridle on his intellect (*Inf*.xxvi.21). Here the Lethe too is presented as a limit over which Dante may not yet cross, a bridle placed on his desires. Like the Pillars of Hercules for Ulysses, it is the boundary of Dante's present quest for knowledge, his exploration of the garden; like the Hellespont, it represents the divine law that proud, presumptuous man must hold his powers in check. Until he has made his confession to Beatrice, Dante is still partly unregenerated; the river reminds him of this and of his present exclusion from full innocence; his inquiring mind, dangerous source of possible pride, must, however unwillingly, be content for the moment to contemplate Matelda and listen to her words of wisdom from the other side of the river.

The first words which the lady speaks to Dante bring together and resolve the two aspects of the garden, as a paradise of pleasure and a paradise lost. She explains to the three newcomers that she does not mourn for man's expulsion from the garden, his true nest, that rather she rejoices in the beauties of nature and the glory of God's creation. Hers is the spontaneous love of the natural world which goes back in Italian literature to Saint Francis of Assisi's *Cantico delle creature* and which Matelda explains in terms of the fourth verse of Psalm 91:

> You have given me joy, O Lord, in your creation, and I shall exult in the works of your hands.

> 'Voi siete nuovi, e forse perch' io rido',
>   cominciò ella, 'in questo luogo eletto
>   a l'umana natura per suo nido,
> maravigliando tienvi alcun sospetto;
>   ma luce rende il salmo *Delectasti*,
>   che puote disnebbiar vostro intelletto.'   76-81

This is to be her function for the rest of the canto, to clear the mists of ignorance from Dante's mind. She picks him out from the group of poets, invites him to ask questions, and says that she has come specifically to answer them, to teach Dante the secrets of the earthly paradise. The question which Dante asks shows that it is Matelda's duty to take over from Statius, who has explained to Dante that there is no weather in Purgatory. Now Matelda will reveal to him the special reasons for the eternal spring of the earthly paradise, the cause of the breeze, the growth of the plants, and the source of the stream.

Matelda's discourse begins with a fascinating circular definition of God as infinite supreme good and infinite love of supreme good: "Lo sommo Ben, che solo esso a sé piace" (91).

This goodness and love were poured into man, whose cause and whose goal is God, supreme good; "fé l'uom buono e a bene" (92). So in the beginning the ultimate goal of man was to be union with God, peace in his will (*Par*.iii.85). In the meantime he was placed on earth, in the garden of delights, as a pledge of this future eternal peace in heaven. But after only a few hours (*Par*.xxvi.139-42) man fell and was cast out from this place of innocent joy and sweet delight, of "onesto riso e dolce gioco" (96) into a world of "pianto" and "affanno", of toil and tribulation, suffering and death.

Matelda confirms that, as Statius has said, Purgatory above the door at the entrance (*Purgatorio* ix) is beyond the region of clouds and storms. The humid vapours, which rise from the earth towards warmer zones of the atmosphere and which cause storms, belong to the lower and middle regions of the air. The garden in which God placed man as a pledge of eternal peace was created in the third or upper region, on the top of a mountain so high that man would not be disturbed or troubled by storms. Yet it is a real garden, as Dante has seen: it has a breeze, trees, flowers, and a stream. These, Matelda explains, are not like their equivalents in the inhabited part of the earth, which depend upon contingent factors of weather, climate, and the seasons, but are controlled, now as in the beginning, by the direct power of the heavens and of God from above. The pure air, eternally revolving with the sphere of the Moon, is broken by the mountain peak, and this causes the gentle, unchanging westerly breeze which brings eternal spring to the paradise. The trees and flowers grow without seed as the breeze carries their creative "virtú" around the garden and from here even to the inhabited earth which thus derives its vegetation, with seeds — subject to contingent factors of place, climate, and season, "per sé e per suo ciel" (113), and so subject also to change and death — from the changeless, seedless, eternal spring of the first Garden, planted by God himself at the dawn of creation. This marvellous process explains and can be confirmed by the fact that sometimes this "virtú" is carried to the northern hemisphere and makes plants grow there apparently without seed. So the earthly paradise, deriving its breeze directly from the motion of the heavens, is both the source and the model of all natural creation; it contains all the plants known to man, but there are also fruits here which man on the other side of the earth cannot know or pick or taste. In this way Dante rationalizes the medieval legends about the Garden of Eden and the impossible theory that it reached up to the sphere of the Moon. He presents the original place of natural beauty, harmony, and peace on earth, not subject to earthly processes of change and corruption, eternally and in a special way dependent on the creative power of God transmitted through the heavenly spheres.

Matelda then explains the river. Its waters do not come from vapours which, rising from the earth, ascend to the cold region of the air and are turned into rain (*Purg.*v.109-11); thus it is not like an ordinary earthly river, subject to contingent events of climate and season, "fiume ch'acquista e perde lena" (123), sometimes swollen and fast-flowing, at other times shallow and sluggish. The source of this river is "salda e certa" (124), steady and undiminishing; God himself directly decrees the existence and the precise size of this ceaseless spring of water which is divided into two streams, to each of which God gives also a miraculous function in the purification of souls before they ascend to heaven. This stream, the Lethe, takes away the memory of sin; its companion, the Eunoè, restores to the soul the memory of good. These rivers, however, are not merely cleansing, like the waters of baptism, they must be drunk. Like knowledge itself, they are the objects of a thirst which must be slaked, and the taste, as Matelda says and as Dante will find out, is of a supernatural sweetness beyond any known elsewhere on earth.

Finally, Dante's wise and beautiful teacher offers to satisfy his other thirst, the thirst for knowledge, by generously adding a corollary concerning the earthly paradise. Although it goes beyond the scope of his question, she knows that it will be

particularly precious to him. So she freely introduces an extra
piece of knowledge to please Dante on a personal level, as a
poet. She tells him that maybe those classical poets who wrote
of man's Golden Age of innocence in a world of eternal spring
among rivers of nectar had their intuition of the truth of the
earthly paradise and its sweet rivers:

> 'Quelli ch'anticamente poetaro
>   l'età de l'oro e suo stato felice,
>   forse in Parnaso esto loco sognaro.
> Qui fu innocente l'umana radice;
>   qui primavera sempre e ogne frutto;
>   nettare è questo di che ciascun dice.'   139-44

This knowledge is mysterious, uncertain, as the "forse" shows,
hidden in the secret springs of poetic inspiration. It is also
imperfect, only a dream. Nevertheless, the recognition of the
possibility that all poets, even pagan ones, might in some
marvellous way participate in an inspired awareness of a
Christian truth reminds Dante of the two classical poets who
have guided him to the earthly paradise. We are reminded of
the presence of Virgil, the pagan poet who yet foresaw the
coming of a new Golden Age, and of Statius, the secret
Christian whose poetry remained pagan (*Purg.*xxii.55-72). The
Christian poet, Dante, turns to see their response to Matelda's
words, and the two classical poets smile with joy at this
"redemption" of some of their poetry (the most beautiful part
and Dante's own inspiration in this canto) from the other
untrue elements, the pagan world of the "false and lying gods"
(*Inf.*i.72).

> Io mi rivolsi 'n dietro allora tutto
>   a' miei poeti, e vidi che con riso
>   udito avëan l'ultimo costrutto.   145-7

Then immediately this brief, innocent, but perhaps still rather
worldly *entente* of the three poets is superseded by Dante's

return to the duties and expectations of his journey as he turns
back to the beautiful lady who tends the earthly paradise and
will look after him until Beatrice comes:

    poi a la bella donna torna' il viso.   148

Notes

¹On the medieval tradition for the earthly paradise and on
Dante's sources for the episode, see the commentaries of
Jacopo della Lana and Pietro di Dante; B. Nardi, "Il mito
dell'Eden in *Saggi di filosofia dantesca*, second edition
(Florence, 1967); A. Graf, "Il canto XXVIII del *Purgatorio*" in
Letture dantesche, II, *Purgatorio*, ed. G. Getto (Florence,
1958), pp. 561-82; A. E. Quaglio's *lectura* in *Lectura Dantis
Scaligera: Purgatorio* (Florence, 1967), pp. 1037-61; P.
Dronke, "Dante's Earthly Paradise: Towards an
Interpretation of *Purgatorio* XXVIII", *Romanische
Forschungen*, 82 (1970), 467-87; U. Bosco, "Il canto XXVIII
del *Purgatorio*", in *Nuove letture dantesche* (Florence,
1966—), V (1972).
²*De Genesi ad litteram* 8, 1, 4.
³The idea of the garland representing fame as well as virtue was
suggested by Benvenuto da Imola in his commentary on the
dream of Leah.
⁴See "Matelda", *Enciclopedia dantesca* (Rome, 1970-6), III
(1971), pp. 854-60; also E. Moore, *Studies in Dante,* third
series (Oxford, 1903), pp. 210-16; J. C. Barnes, "Dante's
Matelda: Fact or Fiction?", *Italian Studies*, 28 (1972), 1-9.
⁵See C. S. Singleton, *Dante Studies 2: Journey to Beatrice*
(Cambridge, Mass., 1967), chapters 10-13; Dronke in his

article cited in note 1 above; Sapegno's commentary on *Purg.* xxviii.40.

[6]This theory was put forward by L. Pietrobono, *Il poema sacro*, 2 vols (Bologna, 1915), I, 91.

[7]See *Conv*.III.xv.

[8]See Buti's commentary on this line.

[9]E. Brown, "Proserpina, Matelda, and the Pilgrim", *Dante Studies*, 89 (1971), 33-48.

[10]See especially the commentary of Pietro di Dante.

[11]Lana and Buti interpret "primavera" as the flowers which Proserpina dropped. See *Par*.xxx.63, but see J. A. Scott's commentary on this word in his reading below of *Paradiso* xxx.

[12]See J. A. Scott's interpretation of "fioretti" in his commentary on *Paradiso* xxx below.

Paradiso VI

J. H. Whitfield

You will remember the warning that Dante gave to us as readers at the outset of the *Paradiso*:

> O voi che siete in piccioletta barca,
>   desiderosi d'ascoltar, seguiti
>   dietro al mio legno che cantando varca,
> tornate a riveder li vostri liti:
>   non vi mettete in pelago, ché forse,
>   perdendo me, rimarreste smarriti.
> L'acqua ch'io prendo già mai non si corse.   *Par*.ii.1-7

("O you who are in little boats, anxious to hear, following my ship which passes as I sing, go back and seek your shores again: do not put out upon the sea, for losing me, perhaps you may remain adrift. The waters which I enter on were never sailed.") Paradise, he means, is not for the likes of us with little understanding. And this lesson is reinforced when he with Beatrice begins to soar aloft from one heaven to the next. Before long he can look down and count out all the activities of men.

O insensata cura de' mortali,
quanto son difettivi silogismi
quei che ti fanno in basso batter l'ali!
Chi dietro a *iura* e chi ad amforismi
sen giva, e chi seguendo sacerdozio,
e chi regnar per forza o per sofismi,
e chi rubare e chi civil negozio,
chi nel diletto de la carne involto
s'affaticava e chi si dava a l'ozio,
quando, da tutte queste cose sciolto,
con Bëatrice m'era suso in cielo
cotanto glorïosamente accolto.   *Par*.xi.1-12

("O senseless cares of mortal men, how far defective are the
syllogisms that make you flap your wings below! Some went
after Law, some [doctors] read the *Aphorisms* [of
Hippocrates], some followed priesthood, some ruled by force
or trickery, some robbery, some civil occupations, some
laboured, wrapped up in the pleasures of the flesh, some gave
themselves to ease, whilst I, set free from all these things, with
Beatrice was up in heaven so gloriously received.") By these
advertisements we should expect in paradise a world of mystic
light, out of our grasp, with Dante turning back his gaze
occasionally, from seven heavens' height, for some withering
judgment on our mismanagement of a sorry world:

L'aiuola che ci fa tanto feroci,   *Par*.xxii.151

("the little patch of earth that makes us all so fierce"). But
Dante's *Paradiso*, whether he realised it or not, by no means
answers to his declarations with regard to it; or rather, though
paradise is what he says it is, his *Paradiso* is by no means all
paradise. The earth he has left behind is not seen at the end of a
telescope, as a worthless bauble to be discarded; whole cantos

and whole episodes are based on human problems and the earthly scene. The most obtrusive of these, the most extensive interview of all the poem, stretching over three whole cantos, comes later on in *Paradiso* xv-xvii in the encounter with Cacciaguida where, far from turning his back upon the earth and bending his gaze towards the *contemplatio Dei*, Dante plumes himself upon his noble birth, counting his family as of Roman origin, enquiring anxiously of Cacciaguida about the state of families in Florence as if his name was Farinata degli Uberti and this was still *Inferno* x.

And here, in *Paradiso* vi, we shall find two inhabitants of paradise, but they and Dante with them are wholly concerned with human things. Perhaps it was a subtle calculation of Dante that paradise would be unbearable for our weak eyes unless we could take pause with the reassuring spectacle of things already known. And perhaps also we must accept the paradox that although from the middle of *Purgatorio* ours has become increasingly a "mondo fallace" which we should do better like Saint Francis to renounce, Dante himself can never cease to regard it as God's world, capable of order if only we get the formulas right. Here we must bear in mind an important revision of dates, which is sanctioned by the most recent edition of Dante's treatise on world order, the *Monarchia*.[1] In the text of this there is a phrase, "sicut in Paradiso *Comedie iam dixi*" (*Mon.*I.xii.6), "as I said before in the *Paradiso* of the *Comedy*." Taken at its face value, the *Monarchia* is the last of Dante's works. In consequence, many, including all those who wanted to leave the idea of Empire behind for the time when Dante has reached in the poem a point of pure orthodoxy, dated the *Monarchia* early on and expunged this phrase as an interpolation in the text. On such an explanation the last editor turns his back since the manuscript tradition shows it is an integral part of the book. And so the ideas on Empire, which Dante first expressed in the *Convivio* in 1307, he still clings to at the end of his life. And, to prove that he had not abandoned them, here they are in any case in *Paradiso* vi.

As his readers well know, Dante sometimes keeps to a
parallel line throughout the separate canticles. *Inferno* vi and
Purgatorio vi are both, like *Paradiso* vi, political. With Ciacco
we have, in the circle of gluttony or greed, the human greed of
the politics of Florence. And in the *Monarchia* for Dante it is
greed which is the principal obstacle to justice. Then in
Purgatorio vi there is the famous lament over the factions of
Italy. And again in the *Monarchia* Dante argues that there
must be a pyramid with at the top the emperor, who is above all
greed and is inspired with all justice. Is it not natural and
logical that in *Paradiso* vi there should be the emperor who
enshrines in two ways the principle of justice?

> Cesare fui e son Iustinïano.   10

In this celebrated line there has been seen mostly the humility
of an emperor whose rank was in the world and now exists no
more in paradise, where earthly distinctions have ceased to be.
"I *was* the Emperor, I *am* Justinian." But we must remember,
too, that habit of mind of Dante which saw names as the
consequence of things. As Beatrice is she who blesses, so
Justinian is he who incarnates justice. This is the sense that
should be given to line 11, against some of the commentators:

> che, per voler del primo amor ch'i' sento,   11

where the "primo amor" which Justinian feels is naturally for
justice, as proved again by line 12, where his love for justice
leads Justinian to codify the law:

> d'entro le leggi trassi il troppo e 'l vano.   12

Now we must not forget that Dante is no historian. The
historian is one who looks back patiently to find, by sifting all
the evidence, what really happened. But even Dante's dates are
wrong. In line 4 he added up to 206 years, "cento e cent' anni e

più", what was only 197. He is concerned with the recipe for getting the next patch of history right. He is looking for the symbols of his theory in the past and he has neither the means nor the inclination to test his theories against the facts. He does not know that though Pope Agapito, "'l benedetto Agapito" (16), came to Constantinople, Justinian probably did not subscribe to the monophysite heresy, which maintained that there was only the divine nature in Christ. And so Agapito did not convert him — "Io li credetti" (19) — and thus inspire in Justinian immediately "l'alto lavoro" (24), the reformation of the *Corpus juris* described here, following on lines 11-12, as "l'ovra" (13). Not only was that a corporative mission accomplished by an army of lawyers for the emperor, but, alas for the cogs of Dante's argument, the dates again are wrong: Agapito was in Constantinople from A.D. 535 to 536 and the reformation of the legal system took five years from A.D. 528 to 533. Dante's sequence is for him a necessary one: for if Justinian had been right in the belief that Christ had one nature only, and that divine, Dante's whole argument on the justice, first of the Passion and then of the punishment for the Passion, would have been invalidated. But the whole providential sequence is Dante's invention, not a historic fact.

Nor is that all that Dante does not know about Justinian as can be seen in the next tercet, with the next "alto lavoro". Or perhaps we should pause a moment and begin again at the beginning. The first imperial name which we shall find in *Paradiso* vi is that of Constantine, who is to be found later on in paradise, and for him there is a remarkable line. He has his place in paradise,

avvegna che sia 'l mondo indi distrutto.   *Par.*xx.60

("Though by his actions the world is destroyed"). This is an allusion to that celebrated and imaginary Donation of Constantine, which Dante can neither disprove nor forgive. It is symbolized here in the unnatural flight of the imperial eagle,

'Poscia che Costantin l'aquila volse
contr' al corso del ciel, ch'ella seguio
dietro a l'antico che Lavina tolse.'   1-3

The heavens revolve in a necessary order from east to west and
the Roman eagle flew with Aeneas, "l'antico che Lavina tolse"
(3), westwards to Rome. But Constantine perverted the course
of nature and took it back to near its starting-point.[2] But also,
note for the eagle, whether in its right seat or in its wrong one,
one of those full and immediate lines, which we can all
understand at once and which satisfy us most in Dante's
poetry:

e sotto l'ombra de le sacre penne   7

("under the shadow of the sacred wings"). This is of course
where Justice reigns; and look through this canto how the
echoes respond to its personification in Justinian: "la viva
giustizia che mi spira" (88); "la giustizia" (105); "la viva
giustizia" (121). "E sotto l'ombra de le sacre penne" (7): this is
for Dante the right order, the just order of the world. He did
not know that the historical detail for Justinian did not fit at
any point. What he had in his mind's eye was the hieratic figure
of Justinian in the mosaics of Ravenna, that and his name,
which is the living embodiment of justice.

And the other "alto lavoro"? Well, you will find it underlying
the line:

e al mio Belisar commendai l'armi.   25

Constantine had undone the work of Providence, reversed the
course of nature: Justinian sends Belisarius, "il mio Belisar" — a
faithful agent, a valued friend — to conquer the Ostrogoths in
Italy and bring the Roman eagle back to its right place. Now
Dante could not read Procopius, who had been secretary to
Belisarius and who commemorated in his history the injustice

of Justinian to his general, an injustice summed up in the vast
picture by David in which the soldier recognizes his former
general in the old blind beggar: "date obolum Belisario".[3]

Justinian then is not a historical figure and there have been
those who have been surprised that he should have got into
paradise. He is a splendid icon, as Dante saw him in mosaic,
and we may transfer our attention to what he symbolizes. The
symbolism comes first in line 4, "l'uccel di Dio", and then it
comes again in line 32, "il sacrosanto segno". Here there is
embodied an attitude of Dante's which began early and lasted
till the end. In the *Convivio* Dante coined the splendid phrase
of the emperor as "lo cavalcatore de la umana volontade"
(*Conv.*IV.ix.10): not any emperor, not Genghis Khan, or
Prester John, or Chien Lung. And still in the *Convivio* there
are those astonishing additions to the theory, where Virgil
speaks *in persona di Dio*, with the voice of God himself, and
offers rule without limit of time or space to Rome; and where
four times Dante repeats in one half-page the same question
about points in Roman history: "E non puose Iddio le
mani . . . ?" (*Conv.*IV.v.18-19). The turning-points in the long
haul towards universal empire for Rome were, in Dante's eyes,
all miracles.

Nor has the vision altered here. First we should notice:

> e chi 'l s'appropria e chi a lui s'oppone,　　　　　33

the reaffirmation of a stance whose most memorable
expression comes in *Paradiso* xvii,

> sí ch'a te fia bello
> averti fatta parte per te stesso.　　　　*Par.*xvii.68-9

Clearly, "con quanta ragione" (31) is irony, as it refers to "chi",
these, in line 33, for these have no reason and Dante discounts
now both Guelph and Ghibelline. He and the Roman Empire
stand in lonely supremacy and he begins again that history of

Rome, studded with real miracles in the half-page of the *Convivio* (IV.v.18-19). Now it is true that the commentators have pointed out that Dante is more modest here in his claims for Rome. He no longer explicitly mentions miracles. But from lines 29-30:

> ma sua condizione
> mi stringe a seguitare alcuna giunta,

from the first moment when Pallas dies helping Aeneas to his destiny in Rome, via for instance the Horaces ("i tre a' tre pugnar" in lines 37-9), who fought "propter iustitiam cognoscendam" (*Mon*.II.ix.15), that is for that Justice which is the banner of this canto and of the Empire, he still enumerates those stages of Roman history which were the staple of the *Convivio* account. And it is still the will of Heaven and the will of Rome which install Caesar as the first Emperor of Rome and of the world:

> Poi, presso al tempo che tutto 'l ciel volle
> redur lo mondo a suo modo sereno,
> Cesare per voler di Roma il tolle.   55-7

One God, one human race, one Emperor, and out of this,

> redur lo mondo a suo modo sereno.   56

Between the cup and the lip, however, there is still something that is not either unity or peace. From line 58 to line 72 we have the dazzling sequence of the victories of Julius Caesar, where the compression has reminded readers of that other dazzling conqueror, Napoleon, in the synthetic vision of Manzoni:

> Dall'Alpi alle Piramidi,
> Dal Manzanarre al Reno,
> Di quel securo il fulmine

Tenea dietro al baleno;
Scoppiò da Scilla al Tanai,
Dall'uno all'altro mar.

"Il Cinque Maggio" 25-30

Not a *mondo sereno* then, but one of swift and crushing
military action, it seems. We must take as commentary what
Dante wrote at the beginning of *Monarchia* II. Once,
superficially observing, he had thought the Romans occupied
the world by no right but only by violence and force of arms.
But when he thought again, he saw it was the work of Divine
Providence and the Roman Emperor, the anointed of the
Lord. And so here in five tercets we have this epic of Caesar, via
the Gallic War to the *De bello civili*, which takes him in
lightning strokes from Spain to Albania and back to the origins
of the Roman eagle,

Antandro e Simoenta, onde si mosse,
rivide e là dov' Ettore si cuba. 67-8

From Antandro Aeneas set sail, while the Simoenta flows from
Mount Ida, through Troy, down by the tomb of Hector, "ad
tumulum, quo maximus occubat Hector" (*Aeneid* 5, 371).
Caesar crosses the Rubicon and Dante has long forgotten
Curio, who gave the fatal counsel and was punished with a
cloven tongue in the ninth *bolgia* of Malebolge. For, as
indicated in the *Monarchia*, Dante has rethought the rise of
Rome and listened to the voice of Virgil speaking in the name
of God. This is a process sanctioned by Heaven and we are
racing forward to its consummation and its fruit. After Caesar,
Augustus, the second bearer of the imperial burden, "quel che
fé col baiulo seguente" (73): he completes the victory, Brutus
and Cassius die for their sacrilege, at Modena he defeats Mark
Antony and at Perugia besieges, reduces to extremities,
Antony's brother; while in Egypt, after the final defeat of
Antony, the wicked Cleopatra kills herself with the bite of the

asp. As far as Egypt the Roman Empire stretches, "al lito
rubro" (79), or if you like, takes in the world, "il mondo" (80).
However we look, said Dante in the *Monarchia*, "non
inveniemus nisi sub divo Augusto monarcha, existente
Monarchia perfecta, mundum undique fuisse quietum"
(*Mon*.I.xvi.1):

> con costui puose il mondo in tanta pace,
> che fu serrato a Giano il suo delubro.   80-1

The process, with Caesar's victories, may have been sharp,
but it was salutary. Not only was Justinian the embodiment of
justice, but so also is the "uccel di Dio", the "sacrosanto segno".
If we doubted it we need only to look on to *Paradiso* xviii and
the apotheosis of this same imperial eagle:

> *'DILIGITE IUSTITIAM'*, primai
> fur verbo e nome di tutto 'l dipinto;
> *'QUI IUDICATIS TERRAM'*, fur sezzai.
>
> *Par*.xviii.91-3

But we should remember also those devastatingly logical
arguments of Dante in the *Monarchia* about this era of
Augustan peace. By them, Christ gave his sanction to the
Roman universal rule by choosing to be born and inscribed in
the census of the Roman world; and then again, by dying under
the legitimate jurisdiction of Rome: "in utroque termino sue
militie" (*Mon*.II.xi.7). Still in the same pages, God and Nature
intended the Roman people for universal empire and therefore
willed the process by which that empire came to power,

> con costui puose il mondo in tanta pace.   80

To Dante's logical mind, to say that Christ chose the moment
of the *pax romana* to be born, is to say furthermore that he not
only sanctioned Caesar's victories, but that he prepared the

noontide of imperial sway.

This may seem suprising; but Dante has another surprise in store in the lines:

> Ma ciò che 'l segno che parlar mi face
> fatto avea prima e poi era fatturo
> per lo regno mortal ch'a lui soggiace,
> diventa in apparenza poco e scuro,
> se in mano al terzo Cesare si mira
> con occhio chiaro e con affetto puro;
> ché la viva giustizia che mi spira,
> li concedette, in mano a quel ch'i' dico,
> gloria di far vendetta a la sua ira.   82-90

In Dante's view of history Julius Caesar is the first Roman Emperor, Augustus is the second and the third one is Tiberius. We may speculate on what Dante would have done with Tiberius had he ever read his Tacitus. But like Justinian, Dante's Tiberius is not a historical figure and mercifully Dante did not make the mistake of putting him in paradise, or even of attaching to him that adjective *good*, which for him belongs to the emperors by virtue merely of their office: "sotto 'l buono Augusto" (*Inf.*i.71). But like Justinian, he embodies universal justice and legitimate rule and presides from afar over that process of the Passion. Had that not been lawful, God's anger with mankind would not have been satisfied. So in line 88 it is "viva giustizia" which credits Tiberius in line 90 with the glory of satisfying the wrath of God with man for his first disobedience.

There follows something which Dante himself finds hard to digest. For if the Crucifixion was right and necessary for man's salvation and is honourable even to Tiberius, why does it, in its turn, need punishment? The answer, such as Dante gives it, is in the next canto where he seeks enlightenment about his doubts. It is a hair-splitting answer and, I hope, not theologically right. It turns upon the same problem we have seen with Justinian's

revised beliefs and shows the relevance of the change in these
within the context of this canto. For we have already seen that
he was converted from the monophysite heresy by Pope
Agapito, that is from the heretical belief that Christ's nature
was divine alone, to the true belief in Christ's dual nature, both
man and God. As man, Christ suffers for all mankind, and that
punishment was right; but to crucify him was also, and at the
same time, an assault on God, the supreme sacrilege. And this
is what Titus punishes in the destruction of Jerusalem.

As I have shown Dante was no historian. He knows that the
Empire is *a priori* right, right and eternal. He fortunately does
not know the shameful curve of its decline. He knows neither
Tacitus nor Gibbon. Instead, he takes a mighty leap from Titus
straight to Charlemagne. He passes over the problem of *which*
really is the Roman Emperor, the continuous eastern or the
new western line. And he reverses the estimate of the Guelphs,
who saw in the consecration of Charlemagne as emperor by
Leo III in A.D. 800 the proper subordination of empire to
papacy. But Dante thought that Charlemagne was already
emperor in 773 when he came to the rescue of Adrian I or was
crowned by Adrian in gratitude for his relief. You will
remember that old joke of the historian Bryce about the Holy
Roman Empire, which was neither holy, nor Roman, nor yet
an empire. But Dante sees here the point of juncture and of
legitimate succession. The pope's line is in the spiritual sphere;
the emperor, whether Caesar, Tiberius, Justinian or
Charlemagne, embodies justice in the temporal sphere and in
this offers protection to the pope. So we come back to those
who presume to usurp the imperial office and who are
foredoomed, whether Guelph or Ghibelline, or the royal house
of France, referred to in the lilies, "i gigli gialli" of line 100, and
Charles II of Anjou, "Carlo novello" of line 106. The answer is
still what it was in the *Convivio* where Dante saw the great
pronouncements of Virgil as spoken with the voice of God,
"quando dice, in persona di Dio parlando: 'A costoro — cioè a
li Romani — né termine di cose né di tempo pongo; a loro ho

dato imperio sanza fine'" (*Conv*.IV.iv.11). In this he echoes the
Aeneid, 1, 278-9:

His ego nec metas rerum nec tempora pono,
imperium sine fine dedi.

And here again he underwrites what Virgil said,

e non si creda
che Dio trasmuti l'armi per suoi gigli!   110-11

Commentators have looked for some special fact of history in
the first line of this tercet or have seen here the warning of
Exodus, a jealous God visiting the iniquity of the fathers upon
the children. But what is essential is the general fact that the
Empire is always right and its opponents, or its apes, always
wrong.

So we come out of the history lesson, not, to repeat the
warning, an investigation into what history was, but a lesson
about what history must be, and we go back to the inhabitants
of this part of paradise. Mercury is the smallest star, yet big
enough for those who sought fame and honour in this world.
And though that noble effort had to be at the expense of the
more essential effort of salvation, so that their beatitude is a
muted one (115-17), yet they acquiesce in their minor share of
bliss:

e quando li disiri poggian quivi,
sí disvïando, pur convien che i raggi
del vero amore in sú poggin men vivi.   115-17

Justinian repeats (but this time and naturally so in this canto in
the key of justice), that nobly eloquent line of Piccarda, which
has often been chosen as their favourite line in Dante by
English-speaking readers,

e 'n la sua volontade è nostra pace.   *Par*.iii.85

This is to be compared to:

Quindi addolcisce la viva giustizia
in noi l'affetto sí, che non si puote
torcer già mai ad alcuna nequizia.   121-3

The warmth of that famous line may serve to show what so far
has been lacking from this canto. It is the *vox humana*. There is
nothing so far to touch the heartstrings. And since the Roman
Empire is no longer even on our horizon we may feel that this is
foreign to us. But suddenly at the tail-end of the canto there
comes a marvellous episode in which people have always been
ready to sense, under the different name, the presence of Dante
himself, though they have not always been able to give a
satisfactory explanation of the machinery by which Dante
casts himself as this old man. I think the explanation is built in,
and that it turns firstly upon the name Romeo that is found in
line 128 for this second inhabitant of the Heaven of Mercury:

E dentro a la presente margarita
luce la luce di Romeo, di cui
fu l'ovra grande e bella mal gradita.   127-9

A *romeo* is not any kind of pilgrim, he is one who is bound for
Rome. This is the hinge; for on the one side it creates a legend
round a historical figure, warped thereby to a quite
unhistorical role. Romieu de Villeneuve was all that Dante said
he was to the Count of Toulouse, except that he was not a
pilgrim but a nobleman and that he was never thrown out of
office by what Pier della Vigna called that harlot envy, vice of
courts (*Inf*.xiii.64-6). But from his name — *nomina sunt
consequentia rerum* —, just as Beatrice blesses and Justinian is
the incarnation of justice, so Romeo,

Romeo, persona umíle e peregrina, 135

comes casually to Provence, advances to the rank of seneschal, restores the fortunes of the county, marries the daughters of his master all to kings and then is cast adrift as an embezzler and goes with noble dignity and nothing but the humble clothes in which he first appeared in the Count's stable as a groom.

But Dante, what has he to do with the legend of Romeo di Villanuova? The connection is, of course, that no one more than Dante is a pilgrim on the way to Rome. He may not have married off the Count's four daughters to four kings. But he has done better still than that. He has written the *Commedia* and given the answer to the problem of world order. And what is his reward? It is to be accused of embezzlement and to remain an exile, wandering precariously through the breadth of Italy. In the story of Romeo,

> e poi il mosser le parole biece
>   a dimandar ragione a questo giusto,
>   che li assegnò sette e cinque per diece,
> indi partissi povero e vetusto; 136-9

you see how that keynote, "a questo giusto", ties Romeo into this canto of "viva giustizia" and Justinian. Then, since it clinches the links between Romeo and Dante, I must quote here that passage from the *Convivio* in which Dante expressed the bitterness of exile: " . . . per le parti quasi tutte, a le quali questa lingua si stende, peregrino, quasi mendicando, sono andato, mostrando contra mia voglia la piaga de la fortuna, che suole ingiustamente al piagato molte volte essere imputata" (*Conv*.I.iii.4). Now looking again at the texts in *Paradiso* vi, one finds:

Romeo, persona umíle e peregrina 135

and

> indi partissi povero e vetusto;
> e se 'l mondo sapesse il cor ch'elli ebbe
> mendicando sua vita a frusto a frusto,
> assai lo loda, e piú lo loderebbe.   139-42

"Peregrino", "mendicando": the key words are in the quotations from both works and all the pathos of this seemingly intrusive episode tells us that it is supremely autobiographical. And if Romeo is "questo giusto" (137), we hardly need the reminder that Dante must here apply this epithet to himself. So we began with the Empire, which is always just, and we end with its chief proponent, who is also just, but is unheeded and traduced, cast out into exile and poverty for his reward. It is not that Dante repents or repeals the message. But he veils, in the legendary tragedy of another victim of injustice, the sadness which he feels in not knowing when the sums will again come right and the order be restored.

Notes

[1] Pier Giorgio Ricci ed., Dante Alighieri, *Monarchia*, *Le opere di Dante Alighieri*, Volume V (Milan, 1965). This is the critical edition in the Edizione Nazionale of the works of Dante promoted by the Società Dantesca Italiana.
[2] Note in line 6 the nearness of Byzantium to Troy.
[3] Jacques Louis David, "Belisarius recognized", Musée des Beaux-Arts, Lille. This picture was exhibited at the Royal Academy in 1972. See *The Age of Neo-Classicism* ([London], 1972), pp. 38-9.

Paradiso XXX

J. A. Scott

Dante is about to reach the final stage of his journey: the empyrean, or tenth heaven, outside space and time, the abode of God and his saints in eternity.

In the twenty-eighth canto of *Paradiso*, the poet had described a vision of God as an infinitesimal point of intense light, surrounded by nine concentric circles representing the nine orders of angels. In *Paradiso* xxix, he holds forth about various theological points and gives a sermon-lecture on the creation of the angels, their faculties and the differences between their various orders, ending with a violent diatribe against the dangerous nonsense broadcast by theologians and preachers on earth, showing Dante sublimely unaware of just how black his own kettle is next to the theologians' pot.

Now, at the beginning of *Paradiso* xxx the poet returns at lines 10-12 to his vision of "the triumph that sports forever round the point which overcame me and which seems enclosed by that which it encloses." Saint Anselm in his treatise on the Trinity compares God to a point, for, as is obvious, a point is indivisible, it has no circumference, and it cannot be measured.

God is *medium punctum mundi*, the point at the centre of the whole universe.[1] This point is truly all-embracing and is only apparently "enclosed by that which it encloses". The vision moves away. And to describe this movement Dante makes use of one of those astronomical similes which appear in other cantos of the poem often to the reader's utter bafflement and which he had first used some twenty years before in one of his *petrose* poems: "Io son venuto al punto de la rota."[2] There is obvious difficulty in finding a different opening for every one of the hundred cantos in the *Commedia* and one must appreciate how brilliantly Dante solved the problem. At the beginning of *Paradiso* xxx, the scope of the poet's syntax is such that it is difficult to follow the thread throughout the comparison, as we struggle with the details of Dante's imagery. But having grasped the whole, we realize that the structure of this overture is very similar to a sonnet with the Italian pattern of eight and six lines. Here, instead, the simile is described in the first nine verses and applied in the last six, making a total of fifteen lines instead of the sonnet's fourteen, which was also a basic measure in the stanza of the *canzone*. Together with the mastery of language, it is these points of technique that show how much Dante had learned during the twenty years of poetic experience he had undergone before embarking on the *Commedia*.

The first three verses set the time: it is just before sunrise. In the *Convivio*, Dante tells us that the earth's circumference is 20,400 miles in length although the miles he uses are medieval Florentine ones.[3] By reading Dino Compagni, we discover that this mile was rather longer than the British mile: about one and a quarter of our miles, in fact, so that Dante is talking about a spot on the earth's surface about 7,500 miles away from the place where "the sixth hour burns" at high noon. This means that it is roughly an hour before the sun rises preceded by "its brightest handmaid", the dawn, which gradually extinguishes the stars "one by one, even to the loveliest". So, Dante's vision fades away and his eyes turn back to Beatrice. There are two things to notice particularly in the Italian, apart from the stylistic atmosphere of Dante's "sweet new style". The first is Sinclair's translation "the mid-sky" for "il mezzo del ciel", where I prefer to take "mezzo" with its technical meaning of "atmosphere" and translate "when the vault of heaven, deep above us . . . ".[4] The second will already be obvious from this phrase, where *deep*, like the Italian *profondo*, is used with the Latin meaning of "high", "deep in the air". In the tenth verse, there is another example of the frequent Latin forms and meanings used in this canto, as the poet seeks the elevation of style and form in keeping with his subject, though Dante is far too clever an artist to keep to a single register or monotone, as we shall see. The words I refer to are "triunfo" and "lude", the latter a pure latinism suggesting the joy and movement of the angels around their Creator. The next line that should be looked at in detail is the fifteenth: "Nulla vedere e amor mi costrinse." This is untranslatable. I certainly cannot give you an adequate rendering; and not even André Pézard really brings it off in his otherwise masterly French translation.[5] Sinclair, however, seems to make it flatter than necessary by stressing the subjectivity of "my seeing nothing and my love": it is especially the second "my" that seems to betray Dante's magnificent line where the "nulla vedere e amor" are so much part of a single thought that they receive a verb in the singular "mi costrinse", while they stress the fact that these are external forces acting on the pilgrim: nothing to be seen, the spectacle is without as well as within, and Love is almost that personified force that had made Dante his slave in the youthful *Vita Nuova*.

However, it is unfair to criticize what is perhaps the best translation of the *Commedia* into English. Instead, I must briefly return to the *Vita Nuova*, as the poet himself does in the following verses. The very word "loda" used in line 17, with the emphasis placed on it in the rhyming position at the end of the verse, must remind the reader of "all that is said of her up to this" moment, but most particularly of Dante's great discovery in the *Vita Nuova*: that central episode where he had found his true vocation as a poet in the eighteenth chapter, which drove him to take as the unique subject of his poetry "those words that praise my lady", thus giving us the magnificent "poesia della loda", as it is termed in Italian.[6] Here, in the *Paradiso*, Beatrice's beauty is such that the poet's task is truly an impossible one. As we already know, the ascent through each heaven produces a corresponding increase in the radiance of her beauty, a gradual revelation of her beatitude, but one which already on three occasions Dante has declared to be beyond his poetic powers.[7] Now he is forced to the conclusion that only the Creator of such a miracle may know and so enjoy her utterly. The poet admits his defeat, "beaten at this pass more than ever comic or tragic poet was baffled by a point in his theme." It is difficult for a modern reader to understand Dante's use of the terms *comic* and *tragic*. Briefly, as expounded in the fourth chapter of the Second Book of the *De Vulgari Eloquentia*, the eclipse of classical drama had divested these two words of the connotations they now still hold after the revival of both critical theory and dramatic practice in the Renaissance; and Dante explains that they are part of a stylistic scale, with *tragedia* indicating a work composed in the most noble style in either verse or prose, *elegia* the lowest style, and *comedia* a mixture between the two.[8] This is why Virgil refers to his "high tragedy" in the twentieth canto of the *Inferno*, though Dante was well acquainted with the *Aeneid*'s triumphant close, and why, in the same area of his poem, Dante himself refers to the latter as his "comedy".[9] In order to describe the whole universe and every aspect of human nature from the bestial to the divine, the Italian poet needed the whole gamut of language, including everything he had excluded from the noble, tragic style of his great *canzoni* in the *De Vulgari Eloquentia*. The latter's range and the conception of poetry expressed in it seem to me to prove conclusively that the *Commedia* cannot have been begun before 1306.[10]

To return for a moment to the translation, it is impossible to reproduce the alliteration in lines 28-9: *vidi-viso-vita-vista*. And it is perhaps important to remember that Italians are on the whole more sensitive to alliteration and more reluctant to use it than we are. When we focus on it, however, we find that the close connection between the words *vidi* and *viso* highlights the fact that the verb "to see" in its various forms appears no less than twenty-two times in this single canto. But more of that later. For the present, the lines make us return once more to the *Vita Nuova*, with its description of Dante's first meeting with Beatrice in Florence "almost at the end of the poet's ninth year" (*VN* II). Here, too, in *Paradiso* xxx the latinisms fall thick and fast: "preciso" (*praecisum est*), "desista", "poetando", and note the difficult rhyme-positions of "poetando" and "terminando", lines 32 and 36, which slow down the movement of the syntax, "tuba" (used by Martial to indicate epic poetry in, e.g., *Epig.* VIII.lvi.4), "deduce" (commentators forget the dual meaning of "to write verses" and "to bring in to harbour"), "ardua" and "spedito" (*expeditus*) "duce": in all, one may count some fifty latinisms in this canto.

Then comes one of Dante's most unforgettable *terzine*, giving the essence of paradise in just three lines:

> luce intellettüal, piena d'amore;
> amor di vero ben, pien di letizia;
> letizia che trascende ogne dolzore.   40-2

Dante's artistry is such that sound and meaning coalesce to give one of the most beautiful and striking descriptions in the whole poem. Strangely enough it is pure description, without any of the poet's superb imagery; yet its sheer music, reinforced by the repetition of "amore" and "letizia" in a manner reminiscent of the troubadours' linking of *stanzas capfinidas*, conveys even to an atheist the beauty of such a vision. The lines have that *suavitas*, that caressing softness of sound which is the hallmark of Dante's *dolce stil novo*; and the repetition of each rhyme word with its own crescendo, forging the links more effectively than any *enjambement*, reaches its climax with "letizia che trascende ogne dolzore", where the use of "letizia" recalls that the word *letitia* had been chosen in the *De Vulgari Eloquentia* as an example of those words in the tragic style "which leave a kind of sweetness in the speaker's mouth", even as the word "dolzore" evokes memories of the troubadours and the joys of Courtly Love.[11]

No theological commentary on these lines is necessary as their immediate impact is enough. But in line 39, where the "greatest body" is the *primum mobile*, the ninth heaven, the largest of the celestial bodies, from which all motion is imparted to the universe, the words "corpo" and "luce" are placed in obvious contrast within the same line, in order to try to make us imagine what the empyrean truly is: paradise, outside the world of matter, beyond space or time, is the mind or the spirit of God, whose primary physical manifestation is light.[12] Books have been written on the light metaphysics of the *Paradiso* and rightly they investigate the important neo-Platonic tradition or remind us perhaps of the Manichean struggle between light and darkness.[13] But a reading of the *Paradiso* must surely send us back to the Bible: "Let there be light" was the divine command necessary for the whole of life and creation. It inspired Michelangelo as well as Dante. And Dante may have been struck by the new Gothic architecture with its yearning for ever-increasing light. He certainly must have been familiar with Saint Paul's resounding phrase: "the king of kings and lord of lords; to him alone immortality belongs, his dwelling is in unapproachable light."[14]

Dante is careful to describe the light he sees as "luce intellettüal": it illumines man's spirit and the angelic intelligences. It is also characteristic of the poetic tone of the final cantos. Even when attempting to describe the indescribable, Dante shows a supreme control of language and ideas that mark him off from the mystics who nevertheless inspired so much of his vocabulary and description.[15] Line 40

also recalls that man's intellect must be activated for him to
love truly. This touches on a great debate in medieval theology:
is love basic to and does it precede understanding, as Saint
Francis and his followers believed, or is it necessary to *know*
before one can love, as Saint Thomas maintained? In this
chicken-and-the-egg debate, Dante follows Aquinas, with a
moderately rationalistic position.[16] And, in *Paradiso* xxviii,
the poet himself makes his position quite clear:

> Quinci si può veder come si fonda
> l'esser beato ne l'atto che vede,
> non in quel ch'ama, che poscia seconda.
>
> *Par.*xxviii.109-11

("Whence you can see that beatitude is based on the act which
sees, and not that which loves, which comes afterwards.") Of
course, at the end of his life Saint Thomas realized the futility
of intellectual knowledge when faced with the infinite mystery
of God's presence, and the pilgrim at the end of the *Paradiso*
will have to follow Bernard, not Beatrice. This is not, however,
to renounce Beatrice's way of knowledge and understanding,
but to complement it, as the ambiguity of Dante's words in
Paradiso xxviii may lead one to suppose: it is "the act which
sees", vision leads to love, greater love. The Beatific Vision
involves the whole man, as far as his capacities will take him.

Now comes a direct reference to Saint Paul in lines 46-51. To
prove the point line 49, "cosí mi circunfulse luce viva", is a literal translation of the Vulgate's "circumfulsit me lux copiosa",
where Saul is blinded near Damascus and converted to become
the Paul who was raised up to the third heaven (Acts 22.6-11).
In his blindness, he had heard the command, "Rise up and go
into Damascus"; and here, Dante, the new Paul, despite his
protestations in the second canto of the *Inferno*, is likewise
prepared for his entry into the Heavenly City.

In line 52, we learn that divine Love keeps this Heaven in its
motionless tranquillity, and our minds flash forward to the

celebrated last verses of the poem where Dante's final words speak to us of "the Love that moves the sun and the other stars." Here, motion is replaced by complete fulfilment of being, and we are also reminded of Saint Augustine's *Confessions*, where, at the beginning, he tells us that our heart is always restless (*inquietum*) until we finally come to rest in God.

Then, in line 53, back to the *Vita Nuova*, where Beatrice's greeting had been evoked with the word "salute" and its double meaning of salutation and salvation: the same is true of Heaven's greeting.[17]

The pilgrim's eyesight is now restored, stronger and more vital than before. He beholds a river of light. The opening "e vidi" is biblical in its tone and solemnity, and the image itself has its counterparts in the Bible. The Book of Daniel (7.10) tells of the supreme judge, "and over from his presence a stream of fire came rushing onward". Isaiah reports (66.12-13): "Thus saith the Lord, peace shall flow through Jerusalem like a river, the wealth of the nations shall pour into her like a torrent in flood; this shall be the milk you drain, like children carried at the breast . . . I will console you then, like a mother caressing her son, and all your consolation shall be in Jerusalem." The last chapter of the Apocalypse (22.1-17) carries the same imagery: "He showed me, too, a river, whose waters give life . . . the Lord God will shed his light on them, and they will reign for ever and ever . . . Come. Come, you who are thirsty, take, you who will, the water of life; it is my free gift", and Saint Bonaventure's commentary is even more specific.[18] For myself, I find an immediate parallel between the river flowing from its source and divine grace which flows from the god-head.

Petrocchi's reading in line 62 "fulvido di fulgore" suggests a reddish-gold brilliance, though Du Cange suggests that *fulvidus* can also mean *impetuosus*, evoking the speed of the river with the brilliance playing upon its waters.[19] The unfortunate ambiguity of Sinclair's translation of line 63:

"painted with marvellous spring" is of course absent from the richness of Dante's "dipinte di mirabil primavera". But we have no time to stop. Immediately our vision is swept on to take in the rest of the description, with the "living sparks" coming out of the river and settling inside the flowers "like rubies set in gold". It was Saint Anselm who had compared God's angels to bees hurrying from the hive to the flowers and back. "Like rubies set in gold": in the next canto, the poet tells us that the angels' wings are golden, while their faces are inflamed with the colour of charity whose warm ruby glow evokes the ardour that inspires the angels in their task.[20] But, again, there is no space for too much detail. For Dante's poetry is very different from the static representations of paradise, with their stylized flowers and precious jewels, such as are found in Byzantine art. Here all is movement and the poet's wealth of imagery changes with kaleidoscopic ease and frequency.

Beatrice tells Dante that he must first drink of the waters before he can understand the reality of the spectacle that has greeted him. The poet had already referred to this water in *Purgatorio* xxi.1-4. It is the water of grace and divine knowledge referred to by Christ in his meeting with the Samaritan woman beside the well: "If thou knewest what it is God gives, and who it is saying to thee, give me drink, it would have been for thee to ask him instead, and he would have given thee living water . . . the man who drinks the water I give him will not know thirst any more. The water I give him will be a spring of water within him, that flows continually to bring him everlasting life" (John 4.10-14). And it will be seen how important the references to water and milk are.

Beatrice goes on to explain that the river, the gems, "the laughter of the flowers", are mere stepping-stones towards the reality of paradise. She calls them "umbriferi prefazi", using two latinisms to convey the idea of what Saint Paul describes as seeing through a glass darkly: a wonderful allegory "shadowy forecasts of their truth". Indeed, we now discover that the whole of *Paradiso* up to this point has been one continuous allegory, as Beatrice had already warned the pilgrim in *Paradiso* iv.28-39. There she had told him that the blessed all reside for eternity in the empyrean; but they appear to Dante in groups in the various heavens, to give him an obvious indication of their relative degrees of beatitude. This, of course, is one of the fundamental justifications for allegory, as Dante goes on to point out. Man's intellect is very limited in its appreciation of purely spiritual truths, and this is the reason why the Bible speaks of God, who is pure spirit, as though he had hands or a face, while it describes angels with human features. We moderns are too impatient to accept such crude attempts to depict things of the spirit; we keep our theology clean of hands and faces, harps and angels, which is perhaps one of the reasons why it makes little or no impact on us. Certainly, it was Dante's magnificent grasp of the need to blend both worlds, the visible and the invisible, that produced the matchless splendour of *Paradiso*, its gradual revelation of supreme spiritual truth, which does not cancel out but complements the world of our senses.

In order to achieve perfect vision, Dante bends down to the water of divine grace. Line 85 records that he did this "to make still better mirrors of his eyes": a perfectly acceptable image for us. But the image held far more for Dante and his medieval audience. They were acquainted with the language of medieval mysticism and philosophy, where the word speculation retained its obvious etymological meaning from the Latin word for mirror, *speculum*. Some medieval writers made a nice distinction between *speculation* in order to arrive at *contemplation* of the truth.[21] More important here, vision through mirrors, *per specula*, was the second stage in the mystic's ascent towards God, where the third and final stage was the vision *in speculo*, in the mirror of the godhead. And to clinch the point, the final lines of *Paradiso* xxix have already referred to God's creation of the angels as forming innumerable "speculi" or mirrors reflecting his image throughout the universe:

'Vedi l'eccelso omai e la larghezza
de l'etterno valor, poscia che tanti
speculi fatti s'ha in che si spezza,
uno manendo in sé come davanti'.   *Par.*xxix.142-5

Dante recounts that the urge to drink was now stronger in him than the desire for milk in a baby awakened long after its normal feeding time. We must avoid any tinge of sentimentality in appreciating the image. Dante's purpose is to imply the essentially *natural*, instinctive drive that compels him, echoing Saint Peter's words: "you are children new-born, and all your craving must be for the pure milk of the word, that will nurture you unto salvation" (I Peter 2.2).

With a baroque image — "la gronda de le palpebre mie" (88-9) — the poet's eyes have hardly touched the water when its shape changes to a circle. Saint Anselm had used precisely the same metaphors to show the oneness of the Trinity: the source, a river flowing out and into a lake, three apparently distinct objects made up of the same substance, water.[22] The flow of the river and its length suggest God's emanation throughout Creation, whereas the circle is a traditional symbol for perfection and eternity, having no beginning and no end.

Then, in lines 95-97-99, comes the cluster of the threefold "vidi" ("I saw"), where the word is made to rhyme with itself (a privilege otherwise reserved in the *Commedia*, four times, for the name of Christ), with the triumphant cry: ("I saw both the courts of heaven made plain", where the word "plain" has none of the solemnity of Dante's "manifeste" charged with the Virgilian "Penates . . . multo manifesti lumine" of *Aen.*3.148-151). It is the great triumph of the true kingdom that the pilgrim now beholds, and I wonder whether we are capable of appreciating the immense nostalgia and yearning present in Dante's descriptions of paradise as "il regno verace" (98), "il paese sincero" (*Par.*vii.130), or at the beginning of the very next canto, "questo sicuro e gaudïoso regno" (*Par.*xxxi.25), the *locus securus* where none need fear.

It is light, too, the *lumen gloriae* surrounding the court of Heaven, that enables the creature to see his Creator and thus find the only form of lasting peace that can satisfy man's being. In line 102 the main stress of the Italian original falls on the word "pace", "che solo in lui vedere ha la sua pace." The word is a hallmark of *Paradiso*. In the fifteenth canto Dante's ancestor came from martyrdom on earth to this peace, "a questa pace" repeating a phrase already found in the tenth canto. Other readings in this volume have already drawn attention to the line which, for T. S. Eliot, contained a typical example of Dante's poetic genius, "e 'n la sua volontade è nostra pace" ("and in his will lies our peace").[23] Here the word comes as a climax to Dante's message in the *Commedia*.

Of the latinisms in lines 109-14, the word for hill, "clivo", was specifically used to denote the most sacred of Rome's hills, the Capitoline, while the word "soglie" (113) retains the flavour of its particular meaning "throne". In line 111, the Italian "fioretti" does not mean young or little flowers, but is on the contrary a collective noun denoting the luxuriant abundance of flowers.

Dante's vision has become superhuman; and in the empyrean the laws of space and time no longer prevail, so that he is able to take in everything (lines 118 ff.). It is what Saint Thomas calls the *simultaneous* vision, without spatial sequence or time lag "unde simul et non successive videntur".[24] The assembly of Heaven appears to Dante in the shape of a rose, which (125-6) "rises in ranks and expands and exhales odours of praise to the Sun that makes perpetual spring". The rare latinism "redole" comes at the end of a series of verbs indicating the immensity of the scene described, and with its *enjambement*, "redole odor di lode" (125-6), continues the upward movement towards God. "Redole" is, in fact, a hapax in the *Commedia*. It is therefore interesting to find that it occurs only twice in Virgil in identical lines in the *Georgics* 4,169 and in the *Aeneid* 1,436, where Aeneas sees with envy and admiration the building of a city, the fulfilment of man's primary function on earth as a political animal: "Even as bees in early summer, amid flowery fields, ply their task in sunshine, when they lead forth their full-grown young, or pack the liquid honey and strain their cells to bursting with sweet nectar . . . all aglow is the work and the fragrant honey is sweet with thyme (*redolentque thymo fragrantia mella*)". Here, too, we are confronted with the sight of a great city, the heavenly Jerusalem, the Rome of which Christ himself is a Roman (*Purg.* xxxii.102), with its bee-like angels taking pollen to and gathering nectar from the flower of heaven, whose leaves enjoy the perpetual springtime of God's sunshine upon them.

Why does Dante choose a rose, which at other times is appropriated for the mystical rose, Mary, Queen of Heaven? It is impossible to give a conclusive answer. But it was the queen of flowers, and its feminine gender fitted in with the idea that the souls of the blessed are married to Christ, the heavenly bridegroom. The glory of medieval rose windows may also have inspired the poet. And even in the field of secular literature, the *Roman de la Rose*, the greatest poem of the Middle Ages before the *Commedia* pointed to the rose's supremacy as the flower of love and was perhaps even imitated by Dante in a controversial sequence of sonnets, entitled *Il Fiore*.[25]

Beatrice takes Dante to the centre, the "yellow of the eternal rose", and asks him to contemplate the great assembly "of white robes". Again there is a reference to the Apocalypse, with John's vision of the "great multitude" standing before the throne of God "clothed in white robes" and the voice from Heaven which tells him: "These . . . have come here out of the great affliction; they have washed their robes white in the blood of the Lamb".[26] And so, the red rose, symbolic of Christ's passion and love for humanity, is turned white, the colour of faith triumphant.

As we have seen, Heaven is also a city. And it would be difficult to overestimate the significance the word held for the poet, exiled from his beloved Florence. His roots were there;

his master Aristotle taught him that life in the *polis* was the highest form of human activity; Dante's fierce love for his native city told him that this was true, with every fibre of his being. But here was an ideal Florence, purified of all injustice and malice: the "City of God" as Saint Augustine had called such a heavenly city in exemplary contrast to, and yet based on, the cities of earth. Hell, too, had appeared as a city, "la città dolente" in the inscription above the gates of Hell (*Inf*.iii.1). It stands as the eternal antithesis of the true city, "la vera città", as Marco Lombardo calls it in *Purgatorio* xvi.96.

The heavenly city is almost full, "few souls are now wanting", as Beatrice observes in line 132. Here the common belief in the forthcoming end of the world that inspired so much early and medieval Christian literature is clear even as it had led Dante to claim in the *Convivio* (II.xiv.13) that humanity had already entered the last stage of history and must await the consummation of time.

After the word "città" the political thread that runs through the whole of Dante's poem becomes most apparent. It is by a breath-taking *tour de force* that the poet manages to end this present vision of Heaven with a further invective against political corruption on earth. It is almost incredible that, at this point in his poem, when his whole gaze is fixed on the supernatural, when his every faculty is engaged in trying to convey the spiritual glory of paradise, when all his thoughts and those of his readers should be turned away from the earth, from this miserable "threshing floor that makes us so fierce" (*Par*.xxii.151), it is incredible that Dante should direct attention to one seat in Heaven, and to one alone, relating in Beatrice's words that it is reserved for the Emperor Henry VII.

Readers of any great work are far too likely to take things for granted. For example, we accept the fact that Leopardi called his poems *Canti*: ever since we first heard of them, they have borne this name. Can we not relive the decision, the act of choice that is a dramatic part of artistic creation? Surely, this is one of the essential functions of criticism: to make us see things for the first time again, to see them as an existential choice. How can critics speak of a final phase in Dante's so-called political thought, in which his "imperialist" phase has been replaced by an "ecclesiastical" one? Are we so bemused by the fiction of Dante's poem that we really believe that he was only God's scribe, a terrestrial reporter who went to the world beyond to interview a number of interesting personalities in the after-life, and happened to come across Francesca, Farinata, Guinizelli, or indeed the empty seat awaiting Henry VII in the court of Heaven? "Only God's scribe" would strike a number of present-day critics as blasphemy; but my words are not chosen lightly: the more you give to the scribe, the more you take away from the poet. Divine inspiration in the *Commedia*, perhaps, but divine revelation showing empty seats in Heaven, no!

We should be surprised, we *must* be surprised by the poet's choice. No other soul is honoured in this way. Popes and others galore were waiting to go to Hell, but no one is singled out for Heaven, apart from a future emperor and of course Dante himself, as can be seen from line 135:

> prima che tu a queste nozze ceni.

Dante turns back from eternity, then, and forward in time to watch the drama played out on earth in years to come. Henry, Count of Luxemburg, was elected Holy Roman Emperor in 1308. To Dante's immense joy, he came to Italy in 1310, accompanied by four cardinals, a token of the absent pope's support for his venture. A year later, he received the iron crown of Lombardy in Milan; and in 1312, was crowned emperor in Rome. By then the pope, Clement V, resided in Avignon, having inaugurated the shame of the Babylonian exile which Dante denounced so bitterly in the nineteenth canto of the *Inferno* (82-7) and in his letter of 1314 to the Italian cardinals. Clement is, of course, the "president of the divine court" referred to in line 142, though the latinism "prefetto" has different connotations from the modern "president", and the

forum of Dante's Italian evokes both the spiritual and political
centre of Christendom, Rome, and the justice that should reign
there and be dispensed from it, the example that should be set
to the rest of the world by Christ's prefect or vicar instead of the
evil ways that corrupt humanity.[27] Clement is accused of
duplicity in lines 143-4. A tool of the King of France, fearful of
the restoration of imperial authority in Italy, Clement finally
turned openly against the Emperor in April 1313, after Henry's
summons to Robert of Anjou, King of Naples, cousin to the
French king, and leader of the Guelph resistance. Henry had
come down to Italy before she was ready to receive him, as the
poet remarks in lines 137-8. He died in August 1313, a broken
man. But God, Dante thunders, shall not long suffer Clement
to remain in "the holy office"; eight months in fact elapsed after
Henry's death in the ironically named Buonconvento. Then, in
April 1314, Clement had to face his eternal judge. The outcome
is clear, according to the last verses of the canto. Guilty of
simony, he will be condemned to the third *bolgia* of the eighth
circle of Hell: "he shall be thrust down where Simon Magus
gets his dues, and shall make him of Anagni go deeper still."

In *Inferno* xix the poet relates that the simonists are buried
upside-down in rock. Simony was the sin of selling the things
of the Holy Spirit for money, its name coming from Simon
Magus, who was cursed by Simon Peter for his blasphemy.
Dante speaks to Nicholas III, as this sin was of course one of
the *péchés mignons* of Peter's successors, and learns that a
shaft in the rock is reserved for papal candidates. The arrival of
Dante's arch-enemy, "quel d'Alagna" (148), Boniface VIII, is
now awaited there. The poet introduced there the name of
Simon Magus, not only in order to curse the biblical inventor
of simony, but more especially to remind us of that other
Simon who was, in Christ's solemn affirmation, Peter (*Petrus*),
the true rock ("pietra", *Inf*.xix.14 and 75) upon which the
Church is founded. This infernal antithesis is also reflected in
the fact that the followers of the wrong Simon, who were yet
the official successors and followers of Peter, are now encased

in the infernal rock, deep in the earth from which the silver and gold they adored were drawn, a reminder of Peter's ultimate sacrifice and humility in choosing to be crucified upside-down. They are also in this topsyturvy position because they had inverted God's moral order by selling the things of the Holy Spirit, which is figured in the flames that lick the soles of their feet in an infernal caricature of the pentecostal flame which descended on the heads of the apostles, just as the sparks, "faville vive" (64), up here, in Heaven, symbolize the spiritual essence of the angels. As a pregnant way of describing Pope Boniface VIII, "quel d'Alagna" (148), draws its power from the irony in the fact that Boniface was born in Anagni, which later became synonymous with the greatest defeat suffered by the medieval papacy, the shame of Anagni, as Dante describes it in *Purgatorio* xx.85-96, where the poet proclaims the wretched pope guilty, through his political machinations and infernal ambition, of goading the King of France into crucifying Christ in the person of his vicar.

Inferno xix is memorable not only on account of the poet's triad of popes, one already *in situ*. It is a turning-point in the *Commedia*, the first canto in which the controversial doctrine of evangelical poverty is preached and Constantine's supposed gift of land and political power to the papacy is bitterly condemned. It reflects the spirit of the *Monarchia*, Dante's controversial Latin treatise, with its sharp reminder to the spiritual vicars of Christ that their Lord himself had made it clear that his kingdom was not of this world. The *Commedia* is not opposed to the spirit of the *Monarchia* as so many critics suppose. *Paradiso* is in many ways a long diatribe against the corruption of the contemporary church, the betrayal of its mission by popes, prelates, monks and preachers alike. Does this mean that Dante has fastened his hopes exclusively on the Church, which he would have reformed as the only guide to salvation on earth? The answer is here, in *Paradiso* xxx, in the seat reserved for an emperor who came too soon. This is the tragedy seen from Heaven. Indeed, in *Paradiso* xxvii.61-2,

Saint Peter himself had spoken of "divine providence which
with Scipio had assured the glory of the world for Rome" and
which must set things right once more; this is quite simply the
language of the *Monarchia*. At the end of that canto, Beatrice
had turned to Dante, reminding him that universal corruption
and anarchy were due to the fact that "no one rules on earth"
(140), there is no effective imperial power because of the pope's
mad ambition and his meddling in temporal affairs.

The basic reason? It is still the same: the diagnosis remains
constant throughout the *Monarchia* and the *Commedia*. It is,
in the words of line 139 of the present canto, "the blind greed
that bewitches you". Greed, one learns in the *Monarchia* is
directly opposed to justice.[28] It is the she-wolf that drives the
pilgrim back into the darkness of the wood in *Inferno* i. The
identification is made in the twentieth canto of *Purgatorio*,
where Boniface's "shame" at Anagni is deplored and where we
are told that this relentless enemy of mankind, "la bestia sanza
pace" (*Inf*.i.58), is devouring the whole world (*Purg*.xx.7-12).
Greed and pride are virtually inseparable for the poet. They are
the all-embracing sins without which man would inevitably
find justice and right order, peace and good government on
earth.

Here, man is compared to an "infant that is dying of hunger
and drives away his nurse." Commentators are generally too
busy explaining the references to Henry VII and contemporary
popes, to notice the fundamental connection that links this
image with the earlier one in lines 82-4. As already pointed
out, the first image was not drawn for any sentimental reason:
its whole purpose was to show the urgency and total
spontaneity of Dante's reaction to the water of heaven offered
him, which he needs in order to grow in vision and
understanding. Like a baby's thirst, it is the most natural thing
in the world.[29] Now the same image returns, but with a terrible
difference. Mankind has become so corrupt that its most basic
instincts are perverted, so that it is like a baby that thrusts aside
the breast while dying of hunger: the most unnatural thing in

the world, man's instinct of self-preservation destroyed. Through the pilgrim's own drinking in line 89 to this final simile, the thread is clear. Dante's purpose is to show that men are now acting in a way contrary to the laws of nature, even to their own nature, corrupted by greed. From Heaven the solution is as simple as the evidence is clear: man only has to understand and follow the natural order to free himself from the dark wood. Like the pilgrim, he will discover how easily and how well everything fits into place, if only he will follow God's plan and not the destructive forces of evil and greed.

So, from the heights of the empyrean, the heaven of fire, a glance is cast back at the depths of the universe, where men have gone utterly astray, catching a last glimpse of Hell, where popes, the spiritual leaders of mankind, have imprisoned themselves in the rock of sin and the fire of greed. Perhaps better than any other, this canto shows the way in which the "sacred poem" is made up of both "heaven and earth", to use the poet's own words at the beginning of *Paradiso* xxv. The centre of paradise itself cannot be described without a brief, but all-important reference to the moral chaos on earth. Politics and morality were not watertight compartments for Dante. They intermingle throughout the poem, and coalesce in the supreme synthesis of this canto. The poet may now go on to describe the reality of paradise in the last three cantos of *La Divina Commedia*.

Notes

[1] St. Anselm, *De fide Trinitatis* IX (Migne, *PL* 158.282-3): "medium punctum mundi . . . indivisibile".
[2] See K. Foster and P. Boyde, *Dante's Lyric Poetry*, 2 vols (Oxford, 1967), I, no. 77 (C in Barbi's edition of the *Rime*), and the commentary in II, 259-64, especially pp. 260-1, "That the

astronomical references are precise (and give a highly probable date for the poem) is characteristic of D: at the same time it is worth stressing that the actual date is quite irrelevant poetically, whereas each astronomical reference is so relevant."

³*Conv.*III.v.11.

⁴Cf. *Par.*xxvii.74.

⁵A. Pézard, *Dante: oeuvres complètes* (Paris, 1965), p. 1637 (lines 14-15): "je fus contraint de ramener mes yeux vers Biétris, par aimer et ne plus voir."

⁶This "poesia della loda" is, in fact, what constituted Dante's "sweet new style", which according to the poet himself began with the great *canzone* "Donne ch'avete intelletto d'amore" (*Vita Nuova* XIX: cf. *Purg.*xxiv.49-51). It has nothing to do with a school of poets or *stilnovisti* invented by nineteenth-century historians of literature.

⁷*Par.*xiv.79-81; xviii.8-12; xxiii.22-4.

⁸*De Vulgari Eloquentia* II.iv.5-6: "Per tragediam superiorem stilum inducimus, per comediam inferiorem, per elegiam stilum intelligimus miserorum. Si tragice canenda videntur, tunc assumendum est vulgare illustre, et per consequens cantionem ligare. Si vero comice, tunc quandoque mediocre quandoque humile vulgare sumatur .... Si autem elegiace, solum humile oportet nos sumere."

⁹*Inf.*xx.113; xxi.2 and xvi.128.

¹⁰The *DVE* is generally recognized as having been written *ca.* 1304-5. For an opposite view on the dating of the *Commedia* (i.e. *Inf.*vi composed before January 1302), see G. Ferretti, *Saggi danteschi,* Florence, 1950, pp. 3-25.

¹¹*DVE* II.vii.5: "Et pexa vocamus illa [vocabula] que, trisillaba vel vicinissima trisillabitati . . . dolata quasi, loquentem cum quadam suavitate reliquunt"; "dolzore" is in fact a Provençal form, used especially by the early troubadours.

¹²See *Par.*xxvii.109 ff.; the *primum mobile* is contained within "la mente divina, in che s'accende l'amor che 'l volge . . . Luce e amor d'un cerchio lui comprende . . . " This "luce intellettüal" transcends the senses and constitutes the *lumen gloriae* of the

blessed that makes God visible to them.

[13]See e.g. G. Di Pino, *La figurazione della luce nella Divina Commedia* (Florence, 1952); J. Mazzeo, "The Light-Metaphysics Tradition" and "Light Metaphysics in the Works of Dante" in *Medieval Cultural Tradition in Dante's "Comedy"* (Ithaca, 1960); E. Guidubaldi, *Dante europeo II: Il Paradiso come universo di luce* (Florence, 1966), esp. pp. 173 ff.

[14]I *Tim.* VI. 15-16: "Rex regum, et Dominus dominantium. Qui solus habet immortalitatem, et lucem inhabitat inaccessibilem . . ."

[15]The point is well made by G. Petrocchi in "Dante e la mistica di san Bernardo" in *Letteratura e critica: Studi in onore di N. Sapegno*, ed. W. Binni *et al.* (Rome, 1974), I, 213-29, and in his recent *lectura* of *Paradiso* xxxi in *Nuove letture dantesche*, (Florence, 1966—), VII (1974), esp. pp. 241-7.

[16]*S. Th.* I.ii.3.1-8; III Suppl.92.1-3; cf. *Par*.xiv.40-2.

[17]See *Vita Nuova* III.1-4, "mi salutoe molto virtuosamente, tanto che me parve allora vedere tutti li termini de la beatitudine . . . conobbi ch'era la donna de la salute, la quale m'avea lo giorno dinanzi degnato di salutare", and the whole of *VN* XI. In the *editio princeps* of 1576, the Inquisitor, Fra Francesco da Pisa, required "la donna de la salute" to be changed to "la donna de la quiete"; and in XI.3, "questa gentilissima salute salutava" became "questa gentilissima donna salutava".

[18]"Flumen aeternae gloriae est flumen Dei, plenum congregatione sanctorum . . . Aeterna gloria dicitur fluvius, propter abundantiam; aquae vivae, propter indeficientiam; splendidus, propter munditiam; tamquam cristallum, propter transparentiam" (quoted by N. Sapegno in his commentary to Dante Alighieri, *La Divina Commedia* (Milan-Naples, 1957), p. 1153); cf. Bonaventura, *Opera omnia*, Volume I (Quaracchi, 1882), pp. 2-3.

[19]Du Cange, *Glossarium* . . . , Volume II (Niort, 1884), p. 625.

[20]St. Anselm's image was first quoted by G.A. Scartazzini in his

edition of the *Commedia* (Leipzig, 1882, p. 822, n. 7): "Millia millium ad complenda patris ministeria, alacri discursu, jugiter meant inter caelum et terram, quasi apes negotiosae inter alvearia et flores, suaviter disponentes omnia", while "rubies set in gold" may well remind us of Dante's beloved Virgil: "qualis gemma micat, fulvum quae dividit aurum" (*Aen.* 10, 134).

²¹See, e.g., Richard of St Victor, *In Ps.* *CXIII* (*PL* 196, 337): "Speculativi sunt qui caelestibus intendunt, qui invisibilia Dei per speculum in aenigmate vident . . . Per contemplativos debemus illos intelligere, quibus datum est facie ad faciem videre, qui gloriam Dei revelata facie contemplando, veritatem sine involucro vident in sua simplicitate sine speculo et absque aenigmate."

²²St. Anselm, *De fide Trinitatis* VIII (*PL* 158, 280-1).

²³ *Par*.iii.85; T.S. Eliot, *Dante* (London, 1965), pp. 46-7.

²⁴*S. Th.* I.xii.10. Resp.

²⁵See G. Contini's important defence of the authenticity of *Il Fiore* in *Enciclopedia Dantesca* (Rome, 1970-6) II, 895-901. Albertus Magnus (*De laud. b. Mariae Virg.* XII.iv.33) gives a good example of polyvalence in medieval symbolism: "Et nota, quod Christus rosa, Maria rosa, Ecclesia rosa, fidelis anima rosa". For the *rosa mystica*, see *Par*.xxiii.73-5 and 88-9. Also Ecclesiasticus 39.17-19, in the Vulgate used by Dante.

²⁶Apocalypse 7.9-14; see *Par*.xxv.94-6.

²⁷The wolf, a symbol of Rome, is also the symbol of greed throughout the *Commedia* reflecting the corruption of justice on earth. The symbol reaches its greatest complexity in St. Peter's denunciation of the "lupi rapaci" who appear "in vesta di pastor" (*Par*.xxvii.55), where the archetypal pope blends the biblical image of the good shepherd with the "lupa" of *Inferno* i and *Purgatorio* xx.

²⁸ *Mon*.I.xi.11: "notandum quod iustitie maxime contrariatur cupiditas, ut innuit Aristotiles in quinto *ad Nicomachum*. Remota cupiditate omnino, nichil iustitie restat adversum."

²⁹See *Par*.xxiii.121-6, where the image of the child at the breast indicates the natural love and gratitude that flourish in Heaven.

Index

851.1
D192zn

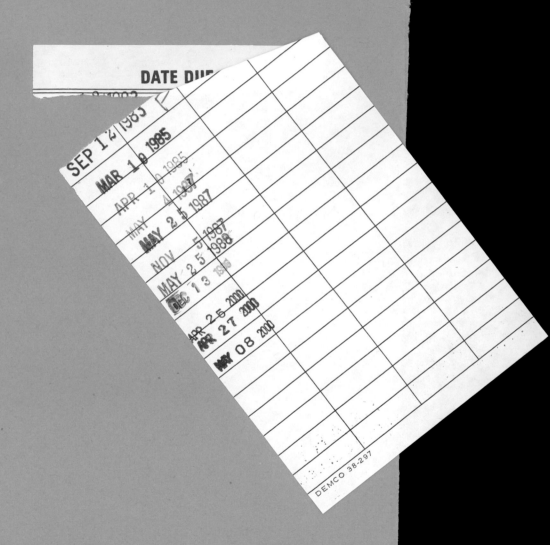

DATE DUE

SEP 12 1985
SEP 19 1985
MAR 19 1985
APR 19 1985
APR 4 1987
MAY 25 1987
MAY 5 1987
NOV 5 1988
MAY 25 1988
DEC 13 1988
APR 25 2000
APR 27 2000
MAY 08 2000

DEMCO 38-297